Oceanborne Madness???

by André Schwartz

Order this book online at www.trafford.com
or email orders@trafford.com

Most Trafford titles are also available at major online book retailers.

Printed in Victoria, BC, Canada.

ISBN: 978-1-4269-0460-8

Our mission is to efficiently provide the world's finest, most comprehensive book publishing service, enabling every author to experience success. To find out how to publish your book, your way, and have it available worldwide, visit us online at www.trafford.com

Trafford rev. 05/20/2010

 www.trafford.com

North America & international
toll-free: 1 888 232 4444 (USA & Canada)
phone: 250 383 6864 ♦ fax: 812 355 4082

Readers remarks:

Dear Andre,

Your autobiographical work is a superb rendition of your life's experiences. It is well written, filled with many anecdotes and a pleasure to read. It clearly shows your innate passion for not only water, sea, but your love of exploring and confronting your findings. It is spontaneous, open, and extremely candid and has a "no-nonesense" approach. You have bared your soul on paper and it is a privilege to have learned a lot from your own experiences in life. Your solo outlook towards life is very optimistic and quite frankly, your approach is perhaps the untouched medical surface that could very possibly cure human depression instead of resorting to chemical cures. Your voyages have widened your scopes, have made you better understand the reasons we are all here on earth. You have shown that nothing is impossible and that if you set your mind on something, achieving your goals while trespassing obstacles CAN be done.

As always, you are a proactive man, always "in motion".

Bravo!

Gabriella Namian

DEDICATION

My two daughters that I know of: Jeannette and Kerstin, the former learned sailing at a very young age and still recalls my many blunders. The people who's path I crossed in good and bad and who contributed to these stories with their being, love and sharing my dreams even when just for a little while and whom I miss on my travels.

ACKNOWLEDGEMENTS

PAUL LAWRENCE WHO'S support and friendship went far beyond friendship when things looked grim and who feels like a brother by choice.

Jim Poushkinsky, another brother by choice and a man who's integrity and unwavering commitment for things that are right, even at risk for life, inspired me to put in words what I believe in. His friendship, editing and proofreading skills make this book readable.

Dave Friesen from S/V Toketie and Brian Ackles of S/V Tarun, more brothers, who inspired me to keep going when things looked hopeless. I will follow their wake.

Gracen Kim, who's knowledge and navigation skills in computers and her permission to abuse her bistro "pvpuerta bistro|café & business center" in Puerto Vallarta marina as a virtual home base and without her patient instructions how to use a computer this book would have never made it to the bookstores.

I'm sure there are others that deserve to be mentioned and despite my excellent memory but regrettably short, have slipped my mind and I ask their forgiveness.

There are many others I have to meet yet and hope to do so before changing tack vertically.

Index

Chapter 1

OCEANBORNE

As I RECALL, it all began on a rainy day in the gutter of the streets of a rural area in a country I found out later was called Hungary.

My assumed parents picked me up and a torrent of sounds reminded me that I was not to be outside in weather like that. Why not never became clear to me even in my adult life. As a child I had always felt strange to go for cover when it was raining, snowing, windy, dark or too bright. Why was it wrong to be outside when it rained or snowed or any weather for that matter? It was fun to feel the water running down my body, the squishy mud between my toes and watching floating objects swirling in the currents as the water rushed toward some unknown destination. Or catching snow with open mouth or letting flakes land on my hand and see them turn into droplets of wetness.

On occasions I was packed into a lot of things to keep me warm, but somehow I still got wet, and cannot remember if I got upset about it. My parents did! They fussed about me saying I would get "monia" (or something like that) and I wondered if that would be a bad thing?

It was all empty promises. I never got monia or if I got it, I never saw it. A few times I had a runny nose and coughed a bit and on those occasions I had to stay in bed and tolerate a glass tube stuck into my mouth that Mother would a bit later remove, look at, and then put a cold, wet rag on my head.

My fascination with running water was taking form in so many ways that it was a good reason for my parents to send me to fetch water from a well about two hundred meters away. We did not have running water and had to fill a barrel with a bucket. It was a lot of going to and fro. By the time the barrel was filled the sun was low.

Saturday was the day we had a bath. We filled a wooden tub with water from the barrel, heated a portion of it in pots on a wood stove, and suffered the burning of our eyes from the soap that got into them. But Mother was happy!

Both of my parents were out of the house most of the time. I had a lot of time for myself, which I spent at a nearby pond with my younger sister. I gathered tadpoles in their later stages when many already had legs, and took them home in jars, putting them into the tub to keep them alive and observe them.

By the next morning I forgot all about them, but was quickly reminded when Mother chased little frogs by the hundreds and wondered where they came from! I tried to rescue a few, but she wouldn't have any of it. She showed no mercy as she swept them outside.

The next day the same happened, but this time she noticed where they came from, and with a swing of the broom caught me before I could take cover under the bed. I don't think my mother had much of a sense of humor, nor did she laugh. I did, before she hit me with that broom!

Following this episode I carried a lot of water to clean the tub, the barrel and the floor from all that was left of the unfortunate frogs. Nevertheless, my preoccupation with water did not diminish. Whenever it rained I snuck out to find a gully or a temporary rivulet, and something that floated and that became my ship. I watched it as it floated on the water, bumped into obstacles, freed itself and continued downstream until it disappeared into a rain gutter or some other hole in the ground, and into oblivion.

Mother observed me when I was about two years old; drawing a bowl shaped something with a line sticking out of it, which had looked like a cross. She was curious what it was and asked. According to her I answered, " A ship." That made her wonder, because there was no way for me to know anything about ships as there are no ships in Hungary of that type, and at that time we lived in the south-east of Hungary with no lakes, rivers or any body of water. Books would have been a luxury so that was out of question, and my drawing remained a mystery for her.

As I grew older I fashioned wood into shapes of boats. They had a mast without sails, and often tipped over because the base did not support the stick and I couldn't figure out how to keep the boat from tipping.

From somewhere came the idea to put something heavy into a hollowed out body and a mast. When I did that, I had in essence built a model Viking ship. It had a square sail and was fantastic. No longer did I allow it to disappear into a gutter. I spent my time on the pond with my new toy. Other boys played with toy cars and balls, I played with my ship and in my fantasy I was in that ship, exploring foreign shores and lived a life of adventure.

Time spent on the water was quality time. With other boys we built raft floats, I even used the tub as boat and my newly acquired skills of swimming added tremendously to my enjoyment.

We played games that had to do with sinking ships from the shore, and we used mud bombs to bombard the occupants of the ships. One was a tub, the one I supplied without my mothers knowledge. I still have no idea how I got it to the pond, but seem to remember dragging it, and carrying it like a turtle on my back, and then again dragging it when it got too heavy. But by golly, it got there! And we used it as our main battle cruiser because it held two of us; one paddling it while the other made and threw bombs back to the shore at the "Bolshevik Ruskies".

After a few sinking, we reversed the roles. The people ashore wanted to be the "Magyar", and the guys in the ships had to be the dirty, mud-eating "Ruskies", trying to invade our homes and steal our home baked potato cakes. Insults flew along with the mud bombs, and in the end the defenders of the land and potato cakes rushed into the water and flipped the boat over, spilling men, mud and words of revenge. But oh, the fun we had! The seed was planted to one day have a boat, and continue the fun. Not even the return of the tub took the fun out of the idea.

Darkness had fallen by the time I arrived at the house we lived in and saw light inside, which meant my mom or my dad were home, and would be wondering where we were. Babysitters were not even heard of then. Kidnappings, murder and all those modern ways to make money and headlines did not exist. Kids in general were left alone to play, and adults were too busy with work to molest us. So we were pretty much on our own, and conflicts among us were solved without the involvement of adults. We learned to get along without the support of a gang, or we just avoided unpleasant encounters.

Talking about unpleasant encounters, here was one to avoid! I thought it better to leave the tub outside under some bushes than to take it inside and reveal it's heroic role in a naval battle. I entered the house to hear: "What…who… Good God, Jesus, Maria and Josef, (for years I thought that was my name), -where have you been? Look at yourself!"

It would have been pointless to explain to them the hardships in a war and the sanitary conditions during those times so I resorted to the best explanation that would make sense and told them "We were playing."

"Where did you get so muddy?" they asked.

How does one explain to civilians who work for a living that making bombs is a dirty business? I shrugged my shoulders and remained silent as my rights allow. That doesn't wash with parental authority, as I was to find out. Water, on the other hand, is a different thing. Looking and not finding the tub, Mother demanded to know where it is and what I did with it. According to the Geneva Convention, I'm not to give out that information, only my name, rank and serial number or so I heard. What followed next was torture, the early equivalent to modern day water boarding. Why weren't camcorders invented earlier, when they were needed? I got smacked a few times, dunked, scrubbed and dunked again under water and then came the punishment; scrubbing the planks. To this day I carry out that sentence. It's been truly said: "No scorn of the Gods is like the wrath of a woman".

Mother escorted me to the well and threatened to drown me. She nearly did, all the while telling me that she deserved to rest when she came home after a hard day at work and not to have more to do when she was home. I bet she never considered what it was like to go through a war and fall into the hands of an enemy and be tortured. In spite of these traumatic events, I ended up in West Germany in the Navy. Here's how it happened.

After the Hungarian revolution in 1956 my parents escaped to West Germany with us, and we all became German citizens. During a vacation my parents visited Kiel, a port town on the Baltic where my fate was sealed. There floated a white ship with three masts reaching for the sky and a materialization of my dreams. Tears obscured my vision and my heartbeat so hard it was hurting. When a sailor asked me why I cried all I could say was "It's so beautiful!" He offered to talk to the captain and if he permitted it, I could come aboard. I almost wetted my pants. Not only did he get permission, but with a senior sailor allowed me to climb up to the crow's nest on the ratlines. The deck and the people looked so small as if they were toys and an hour later when I left, I knew that one-day, I would sail the seas in my own boat.

The drafting system was in effect in Germany and all eligible young men had to serve in the military. At the age of 19 they got hold of me, and my efforts to avoid service in the military did not bear fruit. They asked in which branch I wanted to serve and my love for the water elicited the answer, "Navy!"

"Do you know how to swim?" they inquired,

"What? Don't we have any ships?" I asked. My fear they have all been destroyed during the war must have been all over my face.

The recruiter looked at me with a sadistic grin on his face and said, "Wiseguy, we'll take good care of you and when we're finished with you, you will be this tall. With hat." His thumb and forefinger about a centimeter apart indicated the size. He then made a few

5

notes on his form and my career as a nonconformist in the navy had begun.

I want to skip the details here as much as I can, suffice to say that I managed to get one promotion where others got three, and a psychologist certified me as coming from the mold individualists are made of, in other words, totally unacceptable for military purposes. Where did all this lead? Into a Dojo where I continued the practice of martial arts I had begun before the draft.

Sounds like a contradiction but the way I see it, self-defense is the art of not becoming a victim. It does not necessarily include the creation of victims in the process. People are not taught how to make peace, not even to keep it, but only to enforce it through more violence. It escapes my logic how anybody can think that by beating our perceived enemies long and hard enough we can create friends and peace. It's like fornicating for virginity.

I prefer to share this world with everything and everybody, instead of us all fighting for it like a bunch of starving hyenas. Humanity would be wise to use intelligence to solve problems peacefully, rather than through force. They seem to be the only species carrying grudges. An eye for an eye, and a tooth for a tooth, makes for a world of toothless blind people that will starve without seeing the beauty in the world. Wherever they turn is darkness.

For a while I bogged myself down making money, apprenticed and finished in a few more trades, working as an instructor while taking several courses in various fields and was busy like a one-legged man in a butt-kicking contest. I lived a life like millions of others, but it was not what I wanted, and I thought about going to Canada and living somewhere in the wilderness where I would build a log cabin, hunt and fish, get my pilot's license, and live a life that suited my sense of individuality.

I earned my black belt in Germany in Judo, Tae-Kwon Do, Karate, Kendo and sixth Dan or degree in Jujutsu, and was achieving what as a child I had wanted to be when grown up; An adult, an Indian, a pilot, and live in the Canadian wilderness. The next two things to work on were to go to Canada and learn to fly.

In 1978 I arrived with my very pregnant now ex-wife and we settled in a small town in the prairies not far from the Rockies. Two years later I had my private pilot's license, a baby girl and a divorce. I was now grown up according to some people, but I didn't think so.

Some folks said "You are now such and such an age, it's time to put both feet on the ground." Heaven knows I tried, but I could not even get into my pants that way!

Something was amiss. My daughter and I moved to Vancouver, BC in '86, and I practiced on her my grown up attitude with terrifying and idiotic ideas. To my delight she was resilient to my stupidity, and when I finally wised up instead of growing up, things became much easier. I noticed she was more receptive to what I said or did when I allowed her to be an equal, and became more friend than father.

After two years in Vancouver I took up sailing lessons, and felt like my life started anew. In 1991 I bought my first sailboat, a 26' vessel with a swing keel and a kick-up rudder. It had water ballast that could be emptied to lighten it so it could be pulled on a trailer. A great little vessel to increase my skills and have fun, but she was not a vessel to sail the world with.

When I got her I thought it was all the boat I ever needed and large enough for the two of us. True enough, but a teenager needs to have a boat like the size of the Titanic to feel comfortable on! Being taught by dad was not cool especially when he kept insisting on going sailing when her friends wanted to go to the mall, which was all the time. When I relented to have some of her friends come sailing with us there was a gaggle, a giggle, and a google whenever there was something to be done. What they whispered and giggled about I have no idea, but for sure it was not about how to tack or take a bearing.

As I watched the girls fooling around during a fresh breeze, trying to outdo each other by shouting at the waves, a bigger one hit the side of the boat and dowsed them with a good splash. Listening to them screech and holler like banshees, I asked myself if they would ever understand the ways of the sea, and develop an attitude necessary to sail a boat responsibly and safely?

Today I can answer that question with a resounding Yes! I taught a group of women sailing and they all passed their exam better than their spouses and without breaking things first, but it took two days of answering their questions before we got to sail. The first two days they asked holes into me with whys, how's, and what ifs, but then we got out sailing and things started to pick up nicely. By the time the course was finished, the ladies had all learned their stuff.

For a while I worked for a few sailing schools, and then started to teach independently and decided to buy a bigger boat. Problem is, when you buy a boat and put it in the water, it shrinks. I swear! There should be a label on boats to tell buyers what will happen! The first one was all the boat I would ever needed, but when I threw my jacket below it looked crowded. For sure, she'd shrunk like a wool sweater.

I began to look around, doing research on boats, going to boat shows, and asking owners about boats; what kind, how big, and came to the conclusion that in the end I need to trust myself and be happy with my choice. There are basic considerations as to safety, comfort, and performance, but the rest is learning to adapt to what the boat can do and accepting it. As a Buddhist would say: "True happiness is wanting what you have, not having what you want." My final choice was a 39' French built boat, and with her I am where I want to be at all times.

On her I learned more about myself and although I instructed sailing for several years now on various boats, my learning curve went vertical.

It became apparent where my strength and my weaknesses were, the difference between theory and practical application and where my limits reached their end.

I learned to improvise, invent and explore new ways to make do and patience. Adaptability to changing situations became paramount. Knowledge meant nothing without its proper use, very much the stuff that was not taught in school during my years. It would be hard for me to come up with any comparable activity with similar challenges to ones abilities. Taking responsibilities, becoming self-sufficient and resiliency are the results of living and traveling with a sailing vessel.

Our very survival depends on it because the ocean is still the same in spite of all the new gadgets people are so fond of. In fact, I believe those new gadgets get one in deeper trouble as when they were not available. People were more aware of the risks they faced instead having the illusion of safety with those things.

Chapter 2

ALIEN?

I FALSELY PRESUMED TO have originated on this planet, but that assumption was corrected about the age of four when my alleged parents told me the truth. A stork had delivered me to them from another galaxy, which accidentally dropped me on the Earth.

Reluctantly I admitted the possibility, after observing the predominant species on this planet. Although I looked like them, there seemed to be emerging evidence that I was different. The herd mentality is still very strange to me, as I did not like to be in big groups. Moreover, I don't have the tendency toward self-destruction, and I like to take responsibility for my thoughts, feelings, and actions.

It was a very lonely time while growing into my teenage years. I wanted to be like other kids, but they must have known of my off-world origin, because they picked me last for soccer teams even though I wasn't the worst player. I seldom had more than one friend at a time, and seemed to see things that others did not. For example I noticed that it was not raining between the raindrops, and that a glass filled half full with water was also half empty.

Indeed, a friend of mine got very upset about my observations, and informed me that was the reason nobody liked me. At first I thought he meant they did not like me because the glass was half empty or only half full, but then he clarified that it was because I did notice both, and they did not. Hardly my fault, I thought, all they had to do is to take notice by looking, but it was too late. My reputation as being strange escalated into "weird" and "out of this world" in a negative way. I became known as "the spaced out kid" or "Sputnik" for short.

In order to live with such people I went undercover. I did the same things as them so I would not be discovered to be an alien, although I was not convinced yet of my alien status. As years went by I felt more and more a stranger, and noticed in conversation with others that I was not interested in talk about trivial things. Who was who in the music world or in sports, when and how many goals someone scored, just left me cold. On the other hand, I was interested in discussions about how big the universe is, or when God started his life and who created him. This was definitely not the way to break down my fellow schoolmates' suspicion about me, and reading science fiction stories did not help either.

My popularity was limited to stirring up the teachers, particularly Father Juergen, a corpulent man who was easier to jump over than to go around, and who had a voice that reminded me of the chirping of a sparrow just before the cat got hold of him! The way he moved about in front of his desk in sudden spurts as much as his mass allowed, his head jerking and swiveling on a thick double chin, brought out my cat nature and tempted me to take a swipe at him. His piggish eyes, with heavy bags of dark rings fitting his red thin remnants of hair, were arched in an inquisitive way as he waited for questions he could authoritatively answer.

Except for my questions that is. To this day I'm convinced he would have loved for me to be put in a cauldron with boiling water like a side of pork, so he could watch me squirm. No wonder I put my most challenging questions to him, it was a match made in heaven and the other students loved the way the class went when he and I had our battles. They just sat back or played battleship.

My other victim, our history teacher, loved asking me questions. I answered with a question of my own which he refused to answer, and instead he insisted it was important to remember when Charles

Charlemagne became king of the Franks. I wanted to know for whom it was important. It didn't seem important to me, and what relevance did it have for this moment? The war was on, and we created history instead of digging up bones!

In one instance we had a discussion about borders. My point of view was that borders were artificial man-made divisions because people did not want to share with others what they had, and so created enemies. He rejected this with a wave of his hand; saying "why" was irrelevant because the fact is that there are borders. I replied that that will change with time, and perhaps one day there will be a world without borders. "Dream on", he said, and continued rattling off dates and events. I envisioned a unified Europe when I was twelve, and people laughed at me for saying it. Perhaps it was only a coincidence, but it is almost a fact now. Maybe it was only wishful thinking, or perhaps being an alien allowed me to see into the future?

To my delight I discovered some fellow aliens. They were also working undercover to change this species suicidal attitudes and greedy behavior, by giving living examples and advice on how to live in love and mutual respect for everything and everybody, authentically and with awareness for the benefit of existence. Death and destruction are poor alternatives. How much do we need and take with us, to die satisfied?

I embarked on my journey with a sailing vessel to learn more about this planet called Earth, also known as Gaia and Terra, and found it to be a place of great beauty that is attacked by the greed and ignorance practiced by its occupants and called "progress". They make movies and write sci-fi stories about aliens attacking Earth and invariably are portrayed as the enemy. It's strange to see people looking for an enemy outside of themselves, fighting and killing each other to eliminate their foe, blaming others for their situation instead of looking inward where they would encounter the real enemy. They are destroying the planet they are living on, and it is not an enemy from outer space they need to worry about! They do a great job this far and we couldn't do better even if we wanted to.

This planet is covered with water more than 70% and only about 1% is usable for everything that requires fresh water and the inhabitants are treating it as a garbage dump. Out of sight to them means it is gone. Fact is, all this usable water has been recycled since life on Earth began and in the meantime we put so much garbage into the water, air and soil that the filtering effect has been compromised to an extent that we now need to buy water in stores which has been artificially filtered to be consumable. In many places on this planet, I can assure you, my toilet is cleaner than the surrounding water! Remember: there is no water coming from an outside source to replace our dwindling supply of good, healthy water.

Slash and burn is practiced on land. Clear-cutting destroys habitat for all living beings including humans. Only mechanical robots don't need clean air to breathe. I like calling this planet Aqua-world because there is so much water. Many of those other aliens prefer to be on, near, or submersed in water, so there is a possibility where we come from is a water planet also.

However, I also met a great number of natives to this planet who are using floating vessels and enjoying the waters while adapted to the herd mentality with the attitudes of sheep. They allow others to think for them and to do as they please. This is similar to their land dwelling cousins who are satisfied with solid ground under their feet, and feel secure as long as there is nothing moving. Death is like that, not moving, stable and safe. Death seems to be the most desired condition for many. That might explain the self-destructive tendency. It is very evident in mass-opinions like politics, religions, cultural identities and worldviews. It can be found on football fields, sports arenas, in churches, temples and battlefields. Instead of teaching and promoting individuality, they created institutions called schools and universities where mass conditioning is carried out. Don't move your mind, don't rock the boat, and don't question authority!

Can you imagine the stupidity of priests blessing soldiers going to kill, writing bible verses on guns and bombs and tolerating it? As a matter of fact, it is defended as the right thing on mass media. If that is not the ultimate in religious stupidity and hypocrisy claiming to teach love, I don't know what is.

The galaxy of my alien species discovered individuality as the preferred method of coexistence. We come together as individuals to perform a task that requires group effort. When the task ends, the group dissolves into individuals again, following their own bliss without a trace of herd mentality. We have no politicians, priests, bureaucrats, lawyers or leaders, and therefore are not imbecile followers. We've learned to resolve our issues without the involvement of others who have nothing to do with the problem. We are not looking for who did what to take cheap revenge, but look at the problem and work together to fix it. The problem is the issue, not the person. People can be educated, not problems. We don't believe in punishment or rewards, or in inducing guilt and shame in others. We have no conformists. We keep no secrets from each other, because only the one who knows a secret benefits, and all others are left out. We understand that possessions create thieves therefore we share. There are no wars, no hunger, and no greed. Nobody has more rights because they have more than others; there is no privileged class.

If this sounds utopian, try a different approach to education. First you must educate your educators because ignorant educators can only teach ignorance. Ask yourselves why you'd place belief before knowledge. Believing is easy. All one needs to do is to tolerate being dunked under water and say: "I believe, I'm saved." The only thing you will be saved from is the work required to think for yourself and acquire knowledge.

You know, one man with one eye may lead a million blind but will never follow a million blind. A person of knowledge will transcend beliefs. Remain inquisitive until there is no doubt left. Find out if what you've learned is indeed the truth, or if it may have changed over time. Any person who "knows" has a closed mind. Nothing is certain because everything changes, so remain open. Become role models, teach with your being, and remember, nobody ever learned swimming on dry land. How can you enjoy the sweet fruits of your own cherries if you plant thistles instead of cherry trees? Think about this.

Of course, it is not that easy to shed old habits, and I acquired many of them during my stay on this planet, being surrounded by humans and educated by them. But in the end I remembered that all I have been taught wasn't necessarily the truth. The problem isn't what I was taught; but rather that I believed it. Not that I had much choice. After all I did not have any other aliens around me, and if I did, did not recognize them at that time. It's nearly impossible when society's education puts a blindfold of ideas over one's eyes through which to see the world, and we grow up believing them and thinking we are thinking.

As it turned out, fortune led me to my parents. They had been educated Roman Catholics, and my father had been a soldier in the German army during the Second World War. During his service his beliefs had been shaken off and he questioned everything he heard and thought to be true. My mother still wanted to believe and searched for God in every religion, and found it nowhere. She insisted on me reading the bible every day. So on one side there was my mother who pushed me to read and believe the bible, on the other side was my father who warned me that living in Hungary under the communist regime, I would be subjected to brain-washing in school by listening to the same propaganda every day.

Four years of school in Hungary proved to have been enough for me to recognize (after our escape in 1956 to Germany) that the same thing happened in the church. On top of all that, now my soul was threatened with hellfire for eternity, if I did not believe the teachings of the priest. Siberia sounded better each day!

The questions I asked during religious studies were enough to arouse the suspicions of the priest, who had the ears of God and could sentence me to hell. I stopped caring what would happen when I discovered that he could not answer my questions, and just wanted me to stop asking them so he could continue with his lectures.

At the age of thirteen, after a determined refusal to go to church on my part, I wanted God to punish me with death so my mother would cry over my grave for trying to force me. Challenging God was the ticket. Shouting an insult of the worst kind I could come up with, and believe me, Hungarians have a monopoly on choice words when it comes to insults, I expected a lightning bolt to strike me as swift as a pick-pocket in the streets of Agassiz.

Strangely enough, no lightning struck, but instead I had the sudden recognition that there is no God outside of existence. All of existence, including me, is the same thing. There is nobody to punish or reward me.

This insight opened doors I never even knew were there, and when the police found me and took me home after my parents' alerted them to my disappearance, my mother thought I had a nervous breakdown after listening to what happened, and decided to have our priest look at me. After a 15 minute evaluation of my condition he put his hand around my neck, and with a red face demanded of my parents to have me undergo an exorcism because the devil got hold of me.

As my mother and father were more loving than the servant of God, they took me to a psychiatrist who listened to me for four hours telling him what I did, thought, felt and experienced that night in the park. He then called my parents and inquired from them if I had any Buddhist, Hindu or Eastern philosophy training. Of course not, we are Catholics. Why?

"Well", he said, "what I gather is that the things he says are eastern in concept but I need to see him a bit more to be sure." When they asked what he thought had happened to me, he answered: "Whatever happened to him, I wish it would happen to me!"

That episode of my life is etched in my memory. It has influenced my ways of thinking and observing events around me and has affected my path in life, especially around the issues of freedom, religion and education. When we are taught what to think, that is not freedom. Being taught how to learn is closer to it.

There are laws; civil laws, corporate laws, criminal laws etc. that mostly originate in some religious superstition about moral concepts and conduct. Some are based on common sense, but all are limiting freedom. At least common sense laws are arrived at by common agreements between different people, while the others are imposed.

Take the Ten Commandments; all of them suppress emotional expression. How on earth are you going to explore your potential if you have to stuff it down? How would you know how to correct an error, if you do everything right? How could you know what a mistake is? What is a mistake anyway, and how could you fix it and develop solutions if you won't experiment? We all are making mistakes, and when we use intelligence we learn from them. Too bad only a small percentage of humans are wise enough to do so.

Remember: A smooth sea never made a skillful sailor. We have to have challenges to grow and push the boundaries to discover new things and ways or we'll grow stagnant. Remain inquisitive, it's nature's gift to us.

God never gave commandments, Moses did! It is said: God loves unconditionally so why would he give you commandments? Moses did that because he could not handle his sheep any longer. After 40 years of being too stupid to find his way out of the desert, his control over his flock was slipping out of his hands. He needed a law that cannot be questioned. He had been a lawyer at the court of the pharaoh before his odyssey, and that's what lawyers do, they insist on laws when intelligence fails. Moral of the story: Never leave it to a lawyer to find a way out of the desert!

So what is this lawyer guy to do? Call on a higher authority, that's what they do, even today. Stupid people never cease to amaze me. They are imbued with God's immortality. Nobody dares to question it. I remember a guy who answered me about why he believed in God? "Just in case", he said. Mind you, he kept doing all the things that will take one straight to hell according to the commandments. And so do millions, causing me to wonder why are they going to church and claim to be of any faith? Might as well use that time to make love to someone, at least it will be real fun.

All these fantasy ideologies have not created any peace and I daresay, do just the opposite, but humans cling to it as a monkey to a fistful of peanuts, even though their freedom and life depends on letting go.

There was a guy named Marx who said; "religions are the opiate of the masses" and another one said; "if one has science or art, he has religion". More likely if they don't have science or art, they have religion. On my planet we would choose art and science any day.

When sailing down the coast I ran into some heavy weather, and it put me in danger of losing my life every second for two days, and I remembered a priest saying "there are no atheists in foxholes". How would he know? He was never around those people when they died. How would he know unless they survived and then credited their escape with God's mercy? What kind of hogwash is that? During all those hours of howling winds, crushing waves and life threatening situations not once did I call on God or even though about it. I was too busy surviving.

Someone asked me if I was afraid and I answered no, I was too scared to be afraid. Scared that the boat would break, or that my daughter would be very upset over my lost at sea status. Was I afraid of dying? Hell no! I was more afraid of not living! And live I did, and still do. There will be time enough to relax from living when I'm dead, but I'll refuse to die before I've lived, and there is no better time than NOW to live because there are no other Now.

Death will come to all of us (except to Texans. If they cannot take it with them, they aint goin'!) And we never know when that moment comes so you might as well live now and enjoy every second fully aware, or you'll die regretting not having lived. Unawareness of living is the same as being dead. In an unaware state we hurt each other. Just imagine not having the chance to say you're sorry to someone you hurt before they die. Or imagine you wanted to see the world before you die, and you are dying with a million dollars on your bank account without having done so, because you were too busy piling up the money.

Death is the only certainty and once you fully understand that, you are free to live and be unconcerned about death. She will come regardless of who or what or where you are. Don't act dead while still alive. Live it up!

A Zen student asked his master: "Master how should one live his life?"

The master answered: "By preparing himself for death."

"But how can one prepare himself for death?" asked the student.

"By learning how to live." was the old man's reply.

Robin Williams, playing Patch Adams, used the words in a sense that death is not the enemy, indifference is. Why are we so afraid of death? It's the natural end of life. Let's be prepared for that.

This message is thousands of years old and we still do not understand it. Maybe we teach the wrong messages. Millions suffer fear from countless diseases, and the worst of them all is fear. In fact, fear causes most disease.

Religions induce fear if you don't believe what their leaders want you to believe, and induce hope for an eternal life if you do believe what they say. Some even promise a reward if you do their God's will, according to what they tell you God's will is. And then we are stressed out over which God is real, and what is the true will of Him, Her or It. Nothing kills better than stress.

What a big surprise when you arrive at the Pearly Gates and there are no virgins, no Saint Peter, just an old hag without teeth asking you to give her back her youth. Know that if a God wants something from you he or she will tell you that him or herself. Never let a person tell you what the will of God is. They only want you to further their objectives without putting themselves in danger. Don't be a sheep no matter what they promise you.

Our planet has no sheep, and nobody tells you what to do, what to think, or how to feel. We understand there is no right or wrong, because that would mean there is judgment. Situations exist, and if the situation is undesirable we change it when it is in the interest of all by consulting with each other for the highest good of all concerned, and act accordingly. We may not always come up with a solution that pleases everybody and then we sacrifice our idea in favor of the other and see what happens. There are no guaranties in anything, and knowing that allows for flexibility. That's why life is an adventure, or in the words of Forest Gump's mother, "Life's a box of chocolates". You never know what you'll get.

If I'd known what to expect on my travels, I would never have left. This world is the best so far. I've never learned this much about myself while living on land. There were always others around me whom I'd been busy observing and comparing myself with, and never had time to find out who I was. It took only three days alone in the open sea to find the person I searched for all my life, me.

I watched waves, clouds and the winds and there were no two the same. They mixed and formed other patterns, shapes and appearances, and reality was the result only in the moment, not in the past or the future. Patterns dissolve and form new patterns every second, and even that is too long a time span. It's like observing along a sharp knife-edge, without width.

Other things became clear to me also. The way reality is, or the way I see it, is the interference of waves from many sources. We all contribute, making waves of our own design, and the results of all those waves together create reality. Of course, what I think will affect reality, but so does everybody's thoughts, and the interference of all those thoughts is what reality is. Some are small, others huge but they all contribute to reality, and we are able to affect the size of those waves. We all need to learn about cause and effect so we can make wise choices.

Ah well, these are just my ideas and I will not claim them to be the truth. Surely these thoughts have been thought and observed before, but not by me. For me they are new and therefore significant insights. The good news is; if I can have them, anybody can have them too, and you don't even have to be an alien.

Chapter 3

SAILS vs. POWER

WANT TO KNOW the difference between sailors and power boaters? Presumably both love the water and being on it. But after being on and in and around and above the water while observing others, I'm not so sure. It is so much fun watching children, young and unspoiled by older persons and others as they splash around swimming and jumping and generally just having fun without a goal, versus those who have incorporated competition disguised as fun into their activities.

Now, I have been told that I'm very weird in many ways, and wear it like a price tag on some highly valued item. I'm proud of it. After many years of examining and scrutinizing people and their attitudes I came to the realization that from where I'm standing, they are weird!

First thing I noticed when I went to school was that we had contests in almost anything. There were prizes given to the best, from who read the most books to who could piss higher and farther. Someone had to win and all the others lost. I saw more hanging heads (sorry for the pun) after competitions than flowers after a long dry spell. But we had fun. Well, some did anyway. As soon as awards were introduced into those activities, fun became exclusively the privilege for the winner, and the losers looked for other means to be winners.

Are you wondering yet what all this has to do with sailing and engines? What is the purpose of all this talk about winning and losing? There is one more thing to consider before I come to the point. When did the idea begin that there has to be a winner, and who are these people who uphold the idea of being better than another? How come we think it is important to be a winner? Why do we need to choose sides? Why do we need to go somewhere to have fun, and why do we need to have something to show, like a trophy?

Since I have been a young man once I also enjoyed watching and playing sports but an incidence demonstrated the dangers to live outside of the norm. During a soccer match the guest team scored a great goal and I let out a cheer which has swiftly been squelched with a beer bottle crashing on my head to the roaring laughter of those who had witnessed it. I have always taken pleasure in a good performance regardless by whom and when I see 5 goals I enjoy them all while those who choose sides get to be angry when they chosen team looses and don't get the price they hoped for.

Is it really that important to have something to show? To whom do we need to show it, and why? Do we really need a pile of money for no purpose other than to have it, or a trophy that collects dust?

We even seem to make saving someone's life into a trophy. A person was besting me after I related to a group of friends a rescue I took part in, challenging me how many people I saved because he saved more than a dozen. I couldn't resist replying "Only one whose life really mattered. He saved many other lives by refusing to go to war in Iraq."

Are there any awards for those who loved and shared the best? I think the moment we award anything, that moment we corrupt the deed. Is the result not its own reward?

We make a big deal out of who did or said what, forgetting that the person is not the important part. People die, thank you, but the idea may live on, perhaps for a long, long time.

I have my ideas about those posted questions and I think if you really look around you and go into an inquiring mode, you will find answers that come close to the truth.

So here we have the beginning of the dividing line that I see between sailing and power boating. Be it far from me to think one is better than the other, I would like to say that only the attitudes are different. But hey, things are merging, as is evident in regattas. The fun going sailing is being replaced with the "fun" of winning.

So here is a definition I use often: A power boater gets on his boat and goes where he wants to be. A sailor gets into his boat and is where he wants to be. The emphasis is on being. Could we possibly be joyful without going anywhere, or without triumphing over someone, perhaps even having nothing to show?

I have often experienced how a power boater goes to his boat with a smile, a case of beer and other alcoholic drinks, fishing gear, baseball hat, and usually a bunch of other men, also with baseball hats and more beer and booze. He loads up the gear and other stuff and then heads out into the bay with the obvious intent to have a good time. Where they go and what they do I only can guess, but when they return red faces, stupid grins, watery red eyes, and slurred speech replace the smile. Their voices are loud and boisterous and they are pissed off at the fish who got away just inches before they had them aboard, and admit that the fish outsmarted them. Wow, that tells me a lot about these fishermen's collective intelligence.

Here is where I pause and ask myself, what need was there to go out fishing when their fridge is filled with last week's fish? Was their goal to get drunk? Was it to get pissed off and frustrated because a fish showed more intelligence than a bunch of them? I wonder how many fishermen does it take to outwit a fish? I have come to think that fish, which end up on a boat, must have committed suicide because death was preferable to living in polluted waters. That would show fish are even more intelligent than power boaters who still want to live and fish on a polluted planet.

Why spend so much money to chase fish, come back bitching and complaining, and then tell others what a good time it was? A good time doing what? And if they had a good time, why the bitching? Or is bitching having a good time? Goal orientation and the prospect of some form of reward that has been taught from early childhood and continued throughout our life is the difference. Some of us escaped this conditioning and are then considered by the broken-in masses as weird. Anything outside of their concept of what is normal and of what life is about is strange.

As a sailor, I go to my boat and enjoy fiddling with her to keep her good looking and functional for my own pleasure. Then I take her out to enjoy sailing, including the waves, the wind, the sun, the rain, and going nowhere in particular. I may enjoy a drink but I don't drink to enjoy. We sailors do not complain about "lumpy seas". In fact, when the waves come up we go sailing, and power boaters go for cover! Our fun starts when theirs is finished. It seems that we have fun enjoying life without the goals as such. Our goal is to have fun. The game is what we want to enjoy, not who wins.

I have also observed a trend to win among sailors who I would call power boaters at heart. It is true when there are two sailboats on the water, there is a race, but the race is not about awards, and the result does not leave heads hanging in the wake. It's for the sake of a personal triumph, and not for the satisfaction of beating another. But that is changing rapidly. There is this spreading sickness of egotism, to be number one at any cost. We have the Americas Cup as a prime example of egos at large. Big promotions of companies are displayed, crews are bought to man the ships, and the winners are paid big monies.

Competition is the driving force; awards are the goals, and winning is everything. How can we have fun if we worry about losing? I hear that participation is fun, so why are we not doing it when there is no award to be had?

I believe if we let go of the competing aspect of our life and just enjoy life as it is, the award is the satisfaction of the achievement itself. There is no need for other rewards. Why is it not enough to sail around the world alone or with a crew, and have the experience of doing this as the reward? Do we need to be in the book of records as the youngest, the oldest, the boldest, or the first gay man or woman? Is that not ego talking? Everyone accomplishing something great or even small is contributing to a world of wonder to be enjoyed by all. A janitor in a space agency doing his work is just as valuable as the scientists and their projects because without him or her, the scientists would be working in filth and their work would not be what it is.

Without those fishermen in a powerboat I would not be writing this story. It is time to acknowledge all men and woman equally without grading who has done better than others or who has more. Nobody gets up in the morning saying they will do the worst screw-up today. We all do our best every day, even when yesterday was better. We just want to live to the best of our ability today. Would it not be nice to be seen for our efforts and for who we are, instead of for whom we can beat?

At the time of our death no one will talk about how much money we made or whom we beat. We will be remembered for who we were. Death makes us all equal.

While sailing, I had an experience, which made me look at death as the best friend I could ever have. She taught and showed me that life was not about getting things, nor about accomplishing tasks. Life is about how well I love, and about who I am when living with intensity in the here and now. Instead of worrying about how much I did, my concern is for how well. We would all do well to follow our own hearts rather than what others want or expect from us.

Here then is the answer to the question about sails versus engines. Sailing is using the airflow and our skill to go wherever this combination allows us to go and enjoy. Even if there is no wind at the time, it will come eventually. With an engine no great skills are necessary to force our way to where we want to go as long as the motor is functioning. What more skill does it take to turn a key, push the throttle lever and turn a steering wheel than a six year old could do?

We need something to show, and a fish for a trophy is the usual proof we are grown ups. Granted, there is fun in catching a fish. But when I hear about "Catch and Release" I ask myself why people need to torture a fish to have fun? The fish we catch are exhausted and weak and often injured, and will either become easy victim for other predatory fish or die of injuries if released. And all this is for us to have fun. When I intend to catch a fish, I bait the line and if an edible fish takes the hook, it is dinner. I have been taught young not to play with my food.

In many countries there is a fascination about death, and animals are raised to fight each other for "sport". Bets are made as money is involved in most cases and those attending this spectacle have mixed feelings, being both repulsed and attracted by the brutality of it. In Mexico as well as in Spain people go to watch bullfights and defenders of this activity use flowery words to disguise their thirst for blood and brutality. They will claim it is to demonstrate the superiority of man's intellect over brute strength, and I think those needing to demonstrate that are having a big problem. Cockfights, dogfights, praying mantis and whatever can be used to entertain us on the pretext of "sport" are a form of competing spread all over the world. We like to take credit even when an insect is victorious over another. Is that really the pinnacle of human intelligence?

Nevertheless, it seems to me the sailing community is affected by this trend. I see sailboats heading out with lines in the water, and it is not to supplement their dwindling provisions as much as for entertainment either for themselves or their guests who want to have the thrill of catching a fish. They sure have a thrill when the fish takes the hook and the crew scramble to lower the sails, start the engine and clear the deck. The lucky fisherman gets to play the unlucky fish around the stays, other guests, and the super structure, while handling the rod with frantic encouragement and advice from everyone else.

Oh, it is so much fun to reel the fish in and watch the faces of children and women when the fish has been landed. Now comes the killing that is delegated to someone who has the job to look tough. The fish is flopping around and usually suffocates to death because no one really wants to kill it, and everybody feels kind of sheepish. But in the end we can say that we got something, sailing was not enough. We need to have something to show. Who wants to come back empty handed?

Chapter 4

MIRROR IMAGE

N<small>O MATTER HOW</small> sincere our vows not to treat our children the way we were treated by our parents, no matter how many classes we took in any of the parent preparation courses in anticipation of a new addition in the family, unless we question our established value systems and re-educate ourselves we will never slip out of the straightjacket of our family's educational methods. The situation that brought this insight about began with a math problem my daughter faced in grade two. It put a mirror to my face and an avalanche of memories slammed into me, spinning and sending me into a vortex of emotions and long forgotten childhood experiences.

It started in a window where my reflected image was displayed against the dark outside and a well-lit living room inside, where I was preparing supper and my daughter was doing her homework. The window acted like a mirror, and I acted like an idiot a few minutes later. Allow me to turn back the events a little so you will appreciate the whole story. I will go back in time to age nine when we still lived in Hungary, just before the uprising in 1956.

We lived in a one room dwelling with an outhouse built with boards in the back of the house. The bedroom, kitchen, living room, and dining room were all in one, just like a Swiss Army Knife, and without a mirror. For a long time I had no idea who I looked like, and had to rely on people who said I looked like my dad, while others saw more of my mother, and some jokers claimed to see Attila the Hun. Verification came after we arrived in West Germany and we were blessed with the cheapest toy a 10 year old can get; a mirror. I found out I looked like me, but not exactly.

Those who look into a mirror know what it is like. It is the same except totally wrong. What is left in the image is actually right, when you move your hand to scratch an itch on your back it will be a task to find the spot where the itch is while looking into the mirror. The parting line of my hair was on the right in the mirror, when in fact it is left. I asked my two years younger sister to see for herself, but her hair was parted in the middle so she now had proof that I was nuts. Steering a bicycle by looking into a mirror is suicidal, and will give you good reason to really enjoy life. Try it if you don't believe me.

After we escaped from Hungary, we moved into a two-bedroom apartment in West Germany. We had a mirror on our bedroom wall that was just low enough to see my head, and my curiosity took a strong hold. I began a game of chasing my image and trying to beat him by being the first to appear in front of the frame, however I never succeeded. He always appeared at the same time, looking me right in the eye, and made the same faces at me that I made at him.

It was very frustrating, and I decided to catch him on the other side of the wall and punch him on the nose for making faces at me, but chicken that he was he hid so well I could never find him. I returned to look again and there he was, looking at me and making faces. It drove me insane. Once I took a rock and threw it at him. He had the same idea and I dodged, but my mother aimed better and the target was the real me. I still carry the scar from that well aimed coffee mug.

To drive me completely bonkers, my parents then bought two mirrors, one to replace the broken one, and one for their bedroom. It was on the opposite side over their bed. I reached the conclusion that the other me wanted to play. The bedsprings made a great trampoline, but not a very sturdy one. The two of us proved to be too much for it, and with a funny noise like poi-oi-oi-ngg the springs protruded from the bottom of the bed and made it difficult to hide when my father discovered the damage and chased me with his leather belt.

There was a virtual person in or behind that pane of glass. When I ran into my parent's room, the other me must have taken another route to reach my bedroom because I never once saw him passing me in the hallway, but nevertheless he got there and was looking at me, knowing that all this running and chasing each other will end in some form of punishment, and it did. What I found unfair was that I suffered alone in a corner of my room on my knees saying a thousand times out loud "I will behave and not cause trouble". I lost count many times, usually in my favor, but my parents made sure I counted each line until I collapsed.

I got encouragement from Dad or Mom that they loved me and that hitting me with the belt pained them just as much as me. I begged them to stop loving me because it was hurting too much, but I think they must have been masochists and loved me very much. Oh, the pain they must have gone through. That was when I swore to never allow anyone to love me, and when I had a family of my own not to love him or her either.

Alas, as I grew older the word "love" became a bit confused because there were feelings elicited from actions that did not match the love I knew. I wondered what people meant when they used the word "love" while doing things that actually felt good. I felt this classical contradiction when I read stories in the Bible about a loving God asking Abraham to sacrifice his only son to prove his love. I wondered that God must be very unsure of the love of His children if he needs proof in the form of sacrifice. So when a young woman told me she loved me, I became a bit afraid of her and watched every move she made, ready to run and hide if there was a possibility to get hurt or sacrificed on the altar of love.

Things were good for a while, and then began to fall apart for reasons unknown to me at the time. It was interesting to notice that the girls wanted to get to know me because, according to them, I was different than the other boys. At the age of nineteen I started martial arts training and practiced 5 days a week, and many of the girls were impressed with that and liked my activities.

The Dojo, Japanese for a martial arts training hall, had one wall mounted with mirrors that we used to observe our moves and techniques. I liked the way I looked, especially the facial expressions when I got into the spirit of fighting. Some of the advanced students backed off when I practiced with them, and that seemed to impress the girls. So I began to practice making faces in the mirror to see which face looked the best for a warrior. My looks became that of an adult.

During those "sessions" there was always a feeling of dread and unease. I often felt a dark presence without a face, but ignored it as the price one must pay to be a warrior. My girlfriend on occasions remarked that she felt something like a wall between us, but knew I could protect her. I practiced smiling to attract her, but she insisted I should take things easy.

When we were together she started to complain that I had no time for her. She liked what I did for her and with her, but in the end she left for the same reason she wanted to get together with me. What a dilemma. It never occurred to me that I could have eased off on the training; after all didn't she say she liked me for it?

What did I want to do for more of that good kind of love? Surely not give up training! I needed to do even more, and I joined another school of martial arts. That's what got me her love in the first place, right? Ah, if only I had ears to listen to what was not said! It took many years of broken hearts and a lot of trial and error to hear those unspoken words.

It's funny how mirrors can affect one's life. In my later years I took several courses in personal development, and in one course called "the judgment process" I paired up with a partner to whom I had to say all the things I thought were her character faults, and then the teacher pointed these out as in fact being my own. We tend to project our own stuff onto our partners I was told, and for various reasons blame others and reproach them for our own faults. After reflecting on this for a while I had to admit there was truth in it.

This insight came a little late, since I had already produced two children that I knew about with two women whom I no longer had contact with. For fifteen years I was a single parent. Without the experience of how to handle a teenage girl I was not prepared to be a good father to my daughter, and made all the mistakes that happen with limited understanding. I punished her when I could have just laughed at her antics in using make-up or dressing funny. I sweated with worry and took out my fear on her when she did not come home from her sleepover with friends at the time she was supposed to be back.

She was a great kid, a really great kid! She learned to do many things that other parents considered too advanced for her age like helping build a fence, feeding two horses, cleaning up after herself, painting, making her own sandwiches, washing dishes after meals. It drove me up the wall that she did all these things at the sleepover place, but rarely at home.

At age twelve she sailed a 26' sailboat. She had a blast on a sail down the Frazer River while I tried to kill my outboard engine with my bare hands because it did not want to work. She laughed so hard, she almost fell over the side, admittedly because I gave her a little shove, well, maybe a big shove. That New Years Cruise is still vivid in her memory and she never misses an opportunity to talk about it when we go sailing. The forestay supporting the mast broke the same day when it hit a bridge that was supposed to be open. Never mind the heavy traffic across the bridge. Any fool should have known a mile away that we had a failing engine and were floating down the river out of control. But I'm digressing here and want to go back to her younger years.

In grade two the teacher gave her some math assignments to do at home. They were four rows of ten subtractions, but the crafty teacher jokingly smuggled two additions among them, and when Jeanette solved all of them correctly with the exception of the two adding problems, she came to me for help. In an instant I noticed the plus sign instead of the minus, and when she told me that she could not subtract seven from five I made the most stupid blunder of my life. Telling her that yes, she could do it; she insisted that it is not possible to subtract 7 from 5. I urged her to look again and she still did not notice the + sign. After a moment she came up with "well, is it minus two?" She demonstrated better intelligence than I did, and that's when I blew it.

My fist came down on the tabletop that sent dishes into the air, the cat out the window, and my daughter like a greased monkey into her bedroom. She was no longer looking to find a solution for the problem but for an escape route. In that moment I looked up and saw my father in the window, fury on his face, an expression I knew so well just before the world crashed onto me. I shook with shock and fear, my heart racing like that of a frightened bird, eyes turning liquid as tears obscured my vision; then reasoning returned and in a blinding insight I realized what I had done. My father did the same things, and I never wanted to be like him.

How easy it would have been and how much pain I could have avoided by just pointing out that sign to her. We laugh when we sucker someone into traps like this and no harm is done, so why did I react like an idiot? It was what I learned from my father. We are the mirrors, and if we don't learn to deal with our past and clean up our emotional scars, we will continue this inheritance with our children, and they don't deserve it.

I know you want a happy ending, for me to tell you how I fixed the damage, and I'm sorry to have to say I didn't. Nobody can. The harm we do in causing trauma can't be fixed with ice cream, and in this instance she got both a mental injury and some ice cream. Being nice afterwards does not neutralize the assault. We as potential parents have an obligation to clean up our psychological BS before we have children. Otherwise we remain puzzled why they turn out the way they do, and I can only count myself lucky that in spite of all the horse chips she managed to survive, and I hope turned out to be less burdened than me.

She grew into her teenage years and started to experiment with make-up and fancy dressing and my Fathers view has been that only streetwalkers paint their faces and dress funny and I accepted the same belief without questioning. She just wanted to be beautiful like my girlfriend who used some make-up herself but did not have the skills and finesse.

How can anyone understand a teenager? By the time we have children of our own we have become too "adult" and forget completely how stupid and old-fashioned our parents were, and so continue this tradition. The best we can do is to let go of our assumed responsibility to raise our children into adults. That will happen regardless of what you do. Let them experience the results of their actions, without fixing it for them. That is the love you own them, to be supportive without being the all-knowing parent, and to be a friend. Become that what you want your kids to be, and then see what happens. If you are a phony, they will be phony. Be authentic and they will follow suit. Monkey sees, monkey does, is still a powerful and true slogan.

What you lose when you are always a critic, a nag, and a serious adult who has all the right answers and knows everything, is the connection with your kids, the fun you could have laughing and learning with them, the respect they gain for you when you can admit a fault, admit not knowing, or even acknowledge a painful emotional moment. It took me two viewings of E.T. to let my daughter see me cry. Since that time she knows that I have feelings too. Don't be a stoic; let kids see how you deal with your emotions and how you solve difficult times, that's how they learn.

Remember when a monkey looks into a mirror, it will see a monkey. When a wise man looks into a mirror, he will see a wise man. So look into a mirror as much as possible without an idea of what you want to see, but rather to see what others would see. Someone once said; "I can't hear you, because who you are speaks louder than what you are saying". Don't give good advice, be it.

If your children do not turn out the way you would like, then take a good look at yourself and your immediate surroundings. How real are you? Are you honest even in the most difficult times? Are you pretentious, or are you accepting, reliable, loving, understanding, tolerant, and patient in all your dealings with others and with yourself? Forget religions, they teach obedience, not love. "God will love you when you follow his commandments" they tell you. That is conditional any way you look at it, and true love is freely given without conditions. Even atheists know love. We don't need religion to love. You may believe in a God but let Love be your God, don't let God be your love and forget your fellow human beings over it. And for love's sake, look into a mirror regularly, and don't break it if you don't like what you see. If not satisfied find a way to change the way you are for the better.

Chapter 5

MEMORY LAPSES

W HEN I WAS a little younger, about 50 years ago, my memory was good. It is still very good but so darn short, it defies description. Let me give you a demonstration... Now, what was I writing about?

To my recollection this condition, also known as Alzheimer's disease or Senior Citizen moments (SCM) started when my parents asked me to do something, and for the life of me I could not remember what it was and really had a great moment of "forgetfulness". I then became progressively better until today. I am now in Mexico, or is it Tahiti, (you see, here it comes again) and it is the rainy season here, or at least it rains a lot this time around. As it is very hot during the day, I leave the hatches open for the hot air to be replaced with fresh hot air. There really is no difference in the quality of heat, but it works for the mind. In the night, dark, hot air fills the cabin, and is a great relief. At least one cannot see the sweat washing down the dust from my body and leaving a clean path on the almost believable tan.

Now, what I want to talk about is this blessing in disguises called memory lapse, memory blanks, or something like that. I forget which, but it is like this; after remembering to go for errands in the morning, I look around on the boat, making sure all is where it should be, and remind my cats to remind me what I may forget during my absence. The hatches are open to ventilate the air, and the wind scoop is in place to catch some of the hot wind and guide it into the cabin to keep it hot and fresh. Then after kissing the cats good-bye I swing Tarzan-like up the wall that the vessel is tied to, get my trusty low on fuel bicycle (unless it was stolen over-night) and ride into town. The weather is great. Some clouds in the sky make for a perfect photo, and I will have time to get my chores done before I return to the boat.

The Internet cafe greets me with the familiar message that the server is down with its customary problem. The reliable staff brings me the customary coffee that is reliably cold by the time it gets to me. While I wait for the Internet server to be up again, I fiddle with the lap top, sample the coffee, and sure enough it is just warm. But the waitress is reliably efficient and heats it up in the microwave until it is boiling in the cup and takes ten minutes to cool down again. By the time I remember my coffee, I have forgotten that I had a cup of coffee waiting for me. I have now learned to like cold coffee.

Finally the server is up again; I get my emails and browse through them. Some of the letters require my immediate attention and I answer them, others can wait, and hopefully I will have one of those Senior Citizen Moments that will give me an excuse to forget them altogether. But not long into the waiting I am reminded of the open hatches on Symbiosis by some wet spots appearing on the table and the screen on the computer. In haste I pack up the laptop, put it into the case, and with the intention to reach my boat in a few minutes before it fills with rainwater and sinks, I hurry toward the vessel.

But this intention is like that of good parents who mean well, but have no idea how stifling that is. It is a gauntlet challenge as everybody has taken refuge from the deluge and is intent to slow my progress. Everybody wants to talk to me about my boat, their boat, the neighbors boat and everything else and unless I want to be totally rude, there is no chance to get to the vessel before the rain stops. No explanation short of an outright lie will be accepted, and it is useless to argue with people over the unpleasant prospects of sleeping in a waterbed instead of on one. Even when I was almost drowning in bed and was rescued by a phone call, this was not accepted as a good enough reason to get back without exchanging the latest gossip. All this is not even their fault, as I should remember the many wet nights I spent aboard because of open hatches. However this just seems impossible to remember in the heat of day.

When I finally make it through the marina and find the boat is still floating, my second observation is that the wind scoop has turned into a very effective funnel and is pouring the rainwater into the forward cabin at a rate which would make a professional fire hose look like a child's toy. Of course, the rain stops as soon as I step aboard, like on cue.

My third observation is that I also left the companionway hatch open. That means there is water in the Salon, the cat dish is underwater, and the cats will not be happy about it. You may think big deal, but you don't know my cats. For days they will sniff any food, twitch their tail, and give an accusing look that tells you without sounds and better than any human in his wildest dreams possibly could, just what you can do with that stuff.

I love my cats and am doing all that is possible to keep them on my good side, because when the chips are down they are the ones that keep me sane. I laugh and cry with them and it is amazing how they seem to know when I am at the end of my wits. Those are the times when they drop all aloofness and show their real being, and it would put any human to shame.

But back to the present problem that is the water in the boat. You could say boating would be a dry affair without water, but there are limits to madness, and sleeping in a waterbed does not turn my crank. It will be days before the bunk is dry enough to consider giving it a try. Not to mention the things that now needs to be dried, oiled, and aired, to prevent rot, oxidation and mildew. Consider as well that it is raining almost every day, and you will see the problem. Alzheimer's had its advantages in my youth, but it is definitely a pain in the rear now.

And how do I solve the sleep issue? At night I am mosquito fodder. The cockpit makes a good bed if you are not taller than my height of 167 cm. Then you can sleep athwart ships, which is perpendicular to the direction a ship travels (for those who are not sea-savvy). Of course the heat is up in the high thirties and the only way to get some rest is to sleep in shorts without any other coverings, the perfect offering to the female mosquito populace. I'm surrounded, serenaded, and devoured because of SCM. I always forget to buy repellent whenever I go shopping. No one seems to be as popular and as much in demand as myself, and I believe they have a pet of the year poster of me, wherever mosquitoes live. You can imagine that after a heroic battle to keep them at bay I finally succumb to sleep out of sheer exhaustion, and thanks to Mr. Alzheimer the starving population has a smorgasbord the following night also, and the next.

I must say that this is a kind act benefiting the parent of a brood of starving mosquito larvae, but Alzheimer did not invent forgetfulness to feed hungry bloodsuckers. He was just wondering how folks would go along without remembering the past. This is my story and I'll stick to it. Although in defense of Alzheimer's, I can tolerate folks telling me the same joke several times and still laugh with them. Got to take the good with the bad.

There are other things that make life interesting, and those things seem to grow legs and play hide and seek with me, or else just want to get my goat. Say I'm in the middle of some maintenance work and I need some tools to work with. After using a tool I put it down to get another thing, and then I need that tool again but it has left the building like Elvis. It must have because I cannot find it anywhere. I swear that I have not been in another room, and I'm not crazy. Well, maybe a little. Careful now, don't push it.

So where did I put that tool? I turn things upside down, I search on, in, at, under and every impossible possibility to find it and I don't. I'm losing it. I'm looking everywhere, but this tool has without a doubt cloaked itself and become a Clingon. My Holodeck does not function because I forgot how to operate it, or is "Q" horsing around again? I need to get another tool. I turn and take a step and stub myself, on what? The tool I'm looking for has returned or de-cloaked and is clearly visible half protruding from my foot and my curse is heard in Timbuktu.

Experiencing life like this is fun but painful. Everybody has fun watching this, but the pain is mine. There is no justice in the world. But to my great delight I now have another chance to lose that tool again, without first buying a new one to lose.

Just a few weeks ago I went shopping at a local grocery store. After filling the cart with perishable items that I obviously love to have rot in my boat cooler because I forget to eat it before the foul smell reminds me that I bought it, I could not find my keys for the lock on the bicycle. Here I am with a ton of food in the sweltering heat of the mid-day Mexican sun in my backpack, and two triple-plastic bags in each hand, without the keys to my heavy-duty workhorse. The impression on my face enticed some fellow shoppers to make condescending remarks, something about donkeys and mules and a cab driver took pity and offered me a ride for 200 pesos for a two-minute trip.

To the rescue came two dear friends with a van, which relieved the sweaty cabbie who didn't have to follow through on his hasty offer. We stuffed the goods into the van, and considered uprooting the lantern post and taking it along with the bicycle to the boat, where I have another set of keys just for a situation like this. I decided not to take the post so someone else could use it and have a chance to lose his or her keys too.

A little while later we arrived at the place where the boat is tied between the anchor and the wall, and my friends left. There is some walking to do through a heavy overgrown jungle, including ancient ruins (from the last economic miscalculation of some entrepreneur's dream) before reaching the vessel, and by the time I got to the wall my arms extended to my ankles, and my shoulders sagged to my hips, and I wanted to forget that I still needed to return to the grocery store to pick up my bicycle, but my trusted memory lapses failed me. The goods stowed and the cats fed, I scale the wall again and begin the march to retrieve my chained vehicle.

First things first they say, so I go to a locksmith to get copies of the spare keys. That way I have a spare set to lose again. Then I go back to the store. The lantern post is still there, but not the bicycle. In total disbelief I look at the spot where I left it, thinking perhaps it shrunk or dissolved in the rain that now has begun, or that maybe the bike also has the ability to cloak itself like some of my tools, or that maybe David Copperfield was at work.

Before I curse him and all the thieves in the world, I take a look around in the pouring rain and notice that I'm in front of the store's other entrance, and so the bicycle may be at the other lantern post. To my relief it is! I can safely assume that Mr. Copperfield is on vacation in some other part of the world.

Now memory kicks in again. I think of the boat, and in particular the hatch and the companionway I distinctively remember wanting to close up. My recall tells me without mercy that I forgot to close them when I left the boat. This is the curse of a memory that fails to be reliable. It keeps coming and going at the most inappropriate times, like in the parking lot of a grocery store or some other distant place away from the boat, and creates the agony one goes through thinking about all the water that can enter the vessel before one can get back and close the hatches. Funny how I closed them after the rain got in. Perhaps to make sure it does not get out again, a kind of reverse psychology? So memory lapses have their drawbacks also, and as for now I am glad to have forgotten what it is good for or I'd go completely insane, which already may be the case according to some experts.

Chapter 6

MANGO FRENZY

A H, PARADISE! I traveled 3200 nautical miles for this through the cold North and the windy latitudes around Cape Mendocino and Conception Point. I was overcharged in San Francisco for a repair on the fridge, and lost three sails due to ignorance and high winds (a bad combination if you want to know the truth of it). I endured a long year of hard work under water in San Diego, cleaning barnacles and other stuff off boats whose owners found too difficult to do themselves. Finally I made it to Puerto Vallarta in Mexico, where all my effort was rewarded with fruits I had dreamt about from the onset of the trip.

Not that those fruits were unavailable in Canada, but nothing beats picking the ripe fruit from the tree it grows on, and taking chances to fall off the tree while going out on a limb. Forgetting my age and feeling like a ten year old again is one benefit; the other is being able to pick and choose, very much like the female population during a clothing blowout at a local fashion outlet. Touching, prodding and squeezing is an accepted method to evaluate goods, and anticipation of the sweet juices enticing my palate and running down my chin still gets me into a dreaming state.

Gentlemen, start climbing! If you happen to have a lady friend with you on those occasions, she will enjoy your manly display of astuteness while looking up your pant legs, just as you would look up hers. There are all kinds of fruit in the southern latitudes. You don't have to pick them from the tree yourself, as they are harvested for market before they ripen and stored in warehouses until they mature. However fruits of all kinds that ripen naturally are full of energy and life, and incomparable better in taste than the fruit we buy in stores. Who likes to eat green stuff anyway, unless it's vegetables?

A former girlfriend was very fond of veggies. At a party we attended there was a salad bar, which looked good, and we loaded our plates. A young man whose plate was piled high with enough assorted meats to feed an army chatted with her, remarking that she must be fond of vegetables. She replied, while chewing on a carrot and pointing her fork in my direction: "Yeah, that's why I'm with him." My face must have twisted into the shape of a lemon because she asked for some tea (she loves tea with lemon juice) and he was cured of his infatuation.

After reading these lines to some of my friends, I noticed a gleam in their eyes, so I would like to remind my readers that I'm still talking about fruits. I've considered changing the wording, but the same people insisted I not do so, as it adds a kind of eroticism to the story. Those who do not like it and object are on the path of extinction anyway. Just remember that I really am talking about fruits.

Since the season for mangos just has passed as I write this, I would like to share my experience of a wild runaway fruit chase before I mastered the art of eating a mango. I'm sure there are as many ways to peel and eat fruit as there are ways to skin an animal, but for me it was an arduous and literally a hairy affair. Mangos are harmless until one starts to put a knife to them. I mean, how would you like to be skinned? Would you not try to escape? Sure you would, and so did this mango.

From the moment the flesh was exposed, it jumped out of my hands onto the counter, and from there to the cabin sole. It slithered madly from one side of the boat to the other collecting dirt, human hair, cat hair, ants, the leg of a cockroach, and other assorted critters, with me in hot pursuit.

The mango was determined to get away and rolled with the movement of the boat from one hiding place to another. It went under the table, behind the generator, and just when I had it cornered, it managed to use a lunge of the boat to skip over my hand and was off like a greased monkey toward the cats' litter box, no doubt to make itself as unappetizing as possible.

Horrified, with a desperate twist of my body I cut off its escape route just inches from the intended destination, but alas, the juices left a trail of slippery (and later sticky) coating on the cabin sole. My body's momentum carried me over a floor turned into a skating rink, and I crashed into the plastic litter box, which exploded on impact. Cat litter showered the mango and me. To my relief I had cleaned the box earlier, but the thought of what was happening was still unpleasant

I secured the runaway mango by stabbing it with the knife and impaling it like a vampire, then rose to my feet only to slip again on the floor and land on my rear-end. While holding the mango high over my head with one hand and grasping for anything to support me with the other, I had managed to get hold of the water filter. As I fell the flimsy hose that connects the unit to the faucet broke and water poured on me.

Among some of the choice words voicing my discontent, I discovered some I did not know I knew. Carefully putting my legs under my butt, I regained my footing and took a look at the cause of my predicament.

The mango looked like a hippy in bad need of a haircut, with not only cat hair but also sand and insect parts stuck to it; but I triumphed, even if it was a high price I paid. I had earned the right to call this mango mine and do with it as I pleased, and I did. After replacing the hose to the water filter, I cleaned the fruit, diced it into mouth-sized pieces by holding it with a fork, and with a feeling of revenge, satisfaction, and the joy of a job accomplished, I ate the whole thing. I wonder how my barber knew I had mango for breakfast?

Since that first experience I have developed methods much easier and more efficient for eating mangos, and far less demanding of acrobatic skills. Today I cut the mango in half along the flat side of the stone from both sides, and leave the fruit in the skin. Then I insert the edge of a spoon between the skin and the flesh and carve the fruit out of its skin, using the skin as a dish. This is far more efficient and does not require dishes or plates so I can have mango any place and any time, as long as I have a spoon in my pocket. I have become an interesting character among my friends since they discovered I have spoon and will travel.

For educational purposes it is essential to travel to learn how others do things. Other instructional means like the Internet, magazines and TV will only give you information, not knowledge. Someone once said: "knowledge is power". I think that needs to be clarified. Applied knowledge is power. The rest is only information, and if not used it's like carrying a big rock without any purpose with you when you go for a walk. We can trust that when we need a rock, there will be one, in most instances.

We would be wise to travel light and leave no footprints, so others can enjoy pristine, seemingly untouched, and unspoiled surroundings. We may leave information behind of the things we encountered, but I observe that when tourists go to unspoiled places, developments follow. They want to go for a vacation to get away from the same old stuff, but don't want to leave behind the old habitual conveniences. It's like wanting the mother of your children remain a virgin.

As of late we have discovered that using oil for combustion engines has created a situation where greenhouse effects on the global atmosphere are increasing at an alarming rate. We heard this in Canada more than 20 years ago from David Suzuki in programs like "A Planet for the Taking", "The Nature of Things" and other shows. Al Gore in his great movie "An inconvenient Truth" projects a grim picture if we won't change our ways, yet politicians and lobbyists still insist on drilling for more oil (a .38 cal. gun to the head is not good enough; it has to be a .45!) We are reluctant to use environmentally safer energy because of price. Well, all our savings in money will not save our lives when the planet we live on is destroyed, and the money we saved will not benefit us in the grave. Perhaps it will buy us an elaborate headstone? As far as I know there has not been discovered another planet where we could escape to once we destroyed this one.

Recently the USA has elected a new president who offers hope of change in the States and hopefully in other parts of the world. Are the people ready to support and do their part in his effort to bring about change? It is interesting to watch how people elect someone for change and then resisting the changes. Somewhere I heard this: You can go wherever you want, just don't leave this room. Duh!

I observed in the past that the biggest ideas have been shot down by the smallest minds. It takes a change of mentality and attitude to break away from old habits. Instead of putting the responsibility on some leaders' shoulders, we all must take responsibility for our actions, and not wait for others to do the work for us.

We should take the good ideas of people we meet in our travels and apply them wisely. Instead of missionary work to "save" their souls, try saving our world first! Empty words and hypocritical attitudes only make things worse, no matter what one may believe. Don't take your ideas to other lands with an attitude that you know better. They have survived without you for millennia; perhaps they can teach you something that has escaped your intelligence like the mango escaped my knife. Even a mango can teach you new things if you are open enough to embrace its lessons.

What are missionaries getting out of "saving" souls anyway, kudos from their God and a better place in Heaven than another person? How egotistical can people get? Even in Heaven it does not stop.

If I can find new and better ways to peel and eat mangos, this is proof that we have the capacity to learn and come up with new ways to accomplish things, and not by doing the same things that have brought this planet to the point of destruction with the things we have always done. Let's learn how to eat mangos differently and smarter each day.

Chapter 7

HOSPITALIZATION

A HOSPITAL IS A place to visit if you must, otherwise stay as far away as you possibly can. You could catch diseases or get depressed. Generally only the infirm and doctors go there. But is that not the same thing? You've got to be insane to go to work in a place filled with germs. It's a great place to learn about all the possible illnesses one can have, but only sick-minded folks and those who want to make lots of money have a vested interest to be there. That itself is an infirmity of the mind. As for me, I want to avoid that place like a smoker having a heart attack while thinking it will never happen to him.

On Saturday July 26 '08, I walked down a ramp with my cat cradled in my arms, not thinking of any possible hazard. Suddenly my foot slipped and I fell on my butt. My startled cat raced away, and after a few choice words I saw that my ankle was at an odd angle, and realized it was broken in at least in two places. "Oh great! Tomorrow I have a trip to go sailing with some friends and I break bones!" was my first thought. The second was "how can I do it? How could I go sailing with a broken leg? What if this would happen when I'm on a solo trip in the middle of some Ocean?"

Many years back I fell off a roof and was in the same situation, so now I'm an expert and can tell how it feels like to be limited to one leg. Grabbing my useless foot with one hand and checking what it feels like, I diagnosed that indeed it broke in two places, and I moved the foot out and aligned it with the other bones, putting it in place where it should be. Then I hopped on one leg down to the dock where some discarded pieces of pipe material lay around, and used a length of it for a makeshift crutch so I could get back to the boat. There I could make a kind of brace for the injured foot.

In the meanwhile security from the hotel heard the fall and came looking for me and insisted on calling the ambulance to take a look at the foot, just in case it might be broken. "Old news boys, it is already put back in place and what I need is a brace to keep it from flopping around like a rubber stick."

"And how do you know it is broken?" they wanted to know.

"Look, it bends when I put weight on it. Is that proof enough or do I need to be a doctor to know it?"

They almost fainted when I demonstrated and implored me to stop the performance. I happily obliged because now I felt some pain that until then I had managed to ignore. Because I had no income and no money at hand I did not want them to call an ambulance, but in the end they arrived and I agreed to see a doctor as long as he did not ask for an arm and a leg. We joked and they wanted to know how I knew the bones were broken and I told them that I had experience in that. The security guys assured them as well and told the attendant to ask me for a demo. It was obviously not their ankle.

When we arrived at the doctor's office, a doctor who spoke a bit of English informed me that because I had no insurance and wanted to keep my limbs, (which he could have sold for spare parts) he could do nothing for me. "Fair enough" I thought, "after all he's in it for the money and I don't have any, but now I need to go back to the boat". The ambulance driver offered to take me back for 500 Pesos, and I thought this to be about the most expensive and unnecessary car ride I ever had, but this is a medical truck and they are also in it for the money. Included in the 500 pesos was a cardboard box cut to fit my foot into, and wrapped with masking tape to hold my ankle immobilized. Mexican ingenuity at work.

Back at the marina the security people organized a wheelchair. Six strong men and a young woman escorted me down the ramp to the dock. They fussed over me about how I would get aboard, and made all kinds of suggestions as to what I should do. I opted for my own idea, which upset my tutors, but worked very well. "Let me use my dinghy", I said, "I promise not to use my legs to row the boat". Finally I got into the dinghy, rowed over to Symbiosis and climbed aboard. The worst part was over and I now had time to make plans to sail the boat with all the friends I invited for the following day, and with only 3 hours of sleep. It was then I became aware that it was a bit of a challenge to do this with a fresh fracture.

What the hell, I had two legs, one still working well, so it should be fine! I went to bed at 3 a.m. and got up at seven, started the engine and motored over to the dock. I cleaned the boat and by ten the guests arrived, wondering why I had my foot in a big cardboard box. I explained to them that I prepared for a trip by putting things in boxes, starting with me.

We did have a good time. Some of the guys went diving at a group of islands called Los Arcos, and fed the fish from plastic bottles by squeezing bread through holes in the caps. The divers amused themselves over the feeding frenzy. A friend then offered to take me Monday (the following day) to the local Red Cross for X-rays and sure enough, both the tibia and the fibula were broken, and the doctors in the hospital insisted on using screws and a plate to hold the bones together, reasoning that I was no longer sixteen. They did not know Diddly squat about me, and had a surprise coming. I consented to the hardware, but only if it would guarantee full mobility. That was my mistake. Starving doctors will always take the more profitable road, and they are hungry all the time.

My friend Pepe did a lot of organizing. Paul, another friend, lent me money to buy the hardware, and I made an appointment for surgery Tuesday, July 29 at 0800h. But of course, being in Mexico where they don't know time like the rest of the civilized world and everything happens "tomorrow" it was foolish of me to be there at 0800h. In fact, Tuesday, 0800h could mean anything from January 1 to December 31, any day and any hour. In my case it fell on

Thursday, July 31. It wasn't possible on Tuesday because the doctors went home early due to an important soccer match they needed to attend, and Wednesday could have been deadly for any patient at the hospital being worked on by a severely hung over doctor. So they decided instead to do some serious operations on the local golf course by filling some holes with little white balls. There at least no great harm could happen, unless some white little errant missile created another casualty to be worked on.

In these two days of waiting I learned a lot about hospital society and will attempt to describe the situation without sounding judgmental. Let's begin with the staff. The first thing I noticed was the disinterest and lethargic attitude of the nurses. If they had not had some kind of a uniform, I would have thought they suffered from a disease called narcolepsy, or else they were warmed-up walking dead. The lifelessness that hung around them would have made a mummy look like Van Halen on stage during a Rock concert.

I repeated my name, age, and sex and why I was there every two hours to a squad of them. Finally I started to give information such as naming myself as Pope Paul the Third, no age but a lot of experience, and "ambiguous" as to sex. When they asked why I was there I responded that nothing really exciting happened where I was, so I decided to have a sex change operation to see if there would be more action. These answers got some glitter in their eyes.

Later I found out that they were studying to become nurses or doctors (heaven have mercy on all who fall in their hands) and received no money for their work. It was all volunteer work and practice. That does explain why I had to remove a few stitches myself after the surgery, and why some are still festering.

Now a few words about the "inmates". There were four and because I was never introduced to them I'm forced to give them names according to my impression of them for you to know whom I am talking about. I will call one of them Jesus. It may have been his real name, and he may have been the real one, since he kept on looking at me like I was lost. It was eerie to be observed like a rare exhibition piece during all his waking hours. Not once did he take his eyes off me, not even when they put a needle in his rear end.

He had a pair of glasses that could have served as a magnifying glass for a severely handicapped owl, and his eyes behind them filled out the entire frame and made him appear like a comic figure. He had long, dark hair that could not have been combed for a month, and a beard that would have made an Afghan mountain man happy. I tried to escape his scrutiny by reading a book, but when I stole a look over the edge of the book he still had his eyes fixed on me. Jesus was the easiest of the four to bear.

Then there was Jacko. He must have been picked up in Hollywood where they have them under lock and key for special movies like "House of Zombies", "Revenge of the Brain Amputees" or "Escape from Horror Island".

His bed was just opposite mine. He had a five-gallon bucket beside his bed that he urinated into and drank from. He wore pampers and a gown that he frequently pulled off. His eyes were empty and when he looked at me he did not have half the intelligence of a primate. He moaned and groaned like a lobotomized idiot, urinated into his bed and then went to lay down in another. Sometimes he got up to walk around in the room, then stopped in a corner, dropped his pampers and pissed on the wall.

The wall was not his favorite place though; because he preferred standing in the middle of the room and with the same empty look in his eyes, to just let it go. It took me three calls to the nurses to have them come to take a look when he was drinking from his urine bucket. They scowled at me and disappeared around the corner, presumably to get a new bucket and a mop. But the nurse returned with another person who looked at the mess, then gave me another disapproving glance and walked out. The new person started to tell Jacko that he should go back to his bed, which had not been changed. Indeed, there must have been some intelligence left in Jacko, because he refused to return to his bed and eyeballed mine instead with eyes that did not see me.

With a moan and grunt he moved a few steps toward the shower stall, then entered. I listened to the familiar sound of liquid hitting the floor. Now, there was some reaction from the male nurse. He grabbed Jacko by the arm and tugged him out of the stall, through the room and into the hallway, with Jacko's member pouring urine onto the floor the whole way. When some time later he returned, he seemed to have been sedated because they laid him into his bed, which has been changed while he was gone.

My third companion was a skeleton. When and where they dug him up is hard to say, but I'm sure he would have preferred to stay where he was rather than be subjected to the living. His breathing was a death rattle with a variable pitch that kept everybody awake, and continually reminded us of the impermanence of all there is. The nurses loved him because it gave them a job to do; the doctors loved him because there was nothing they had to do with him to make money. Well, I'm not sure about that, but people who came to see the skeleton were dressed very well. Either they came from a wedding or the opera. I observed a doctor with a long face leaving with one of the visitors of the skeleton, and returning with a smile so wide he could have chewed on both of his ears.

The next day the skeleton was prodded, turned over, and a thermometer inserted. Then he was hooked up to a machine that I thought was borrowed from Dr. Frankenstein. The death rattle continued through the night with an intensity that brought some of the dead back to life to see what that noise was all about.

I managed to pass out for a time, but have no recollection how long, when a horrible silence broke out. I awakened asking myself "What? What happened?" It became apparent the skeleton had put an end to all the activity centered on him by having the mercy to die and put us out of our misery by doing so. I see where skeletons have more humaneness than some of the living.

The fourth inmate was in pain. It must have been the worst pain in the world because he asked for pills every 10 minutes. The IV hanging on his bed seemed not to have been enough and his arm in a sling indicated an injury that made him use the bedpan instead of the bathroom. Perhaps the young nurse convinced him of the necessity to use it because she assisted him several times or possibly the fresh tattoos caused all that pain and put him into an agony that was out of this world.

He complained about the food, the service, the nurses, the doctors, the other inmates, God and the Universe. We asked the nurses to give him some sleeping pills and they must have seen the advantage of that as about 15 minutes later the young man was sound asleep for most of the day.

It was a Thursday then and the procedure to get my surgery began with the usual questions. What happened, how did it happen, why, name, age, gender, religion and the purpose of me being there?

I made some correction to my previous statement about a sex change operation and they made a note of that. Then off we went. To my relief they took an X-ray of my ankle. Then they gave me a needle with something in it that made me sleepy, and told me to count. By that time I had forgotten numbers.

When I awoke I was back in my room with a huge bundle around my ankle and a book on my chest. Pepe was sitting on the chair. I checked quickly on my gender status, and to my satisfaction all seemed to be in place. Pepe and I made plans to leave the next day and it was granted with the condition that I came back to have the stitches removed in a week. "Don't put any weight on your leg for at least eight weeks" they told me, "and take the pain medication". I did take the pills, and put them in a safe place where they would do no harm.

A week later I rode my bicycle 10 miles (16km) to the hospital and they removed half of the stitches and promised to remove the rest the next day. I wondered why they needed to take my blood pressure? The nurse expressed concern about my pulse to the doctor. He was happy about my blood pressure and made a remark about it being better than any young person in good shape, but added that my pulse was too slow. When I explained to him that during meditation I could get my pulse as slow as 22 beats per minute, he objected saying it was very dangerous and I shouldn't do that.

I replied, "Doc, because of meditating for many years I find no problems with my heart and heal much faster than expected. In fact, I will be walking on my feet probably in a few days".

He insisted, "That would take a miracle. You are not 16. Even then it would take a minimum 6 weeks. You have seven screws and a plate to hold the bones together."

"You please take care of the stitches doc, I will take care of the miracles", I answered, and to prove my point I returned with the bicycle the next day without crutches on my own feet. I was limping of course, but no crutches. There are more witnesses still alive today to testify to that, than there were Christians who could claim to have witnessed the resurrection of Jesus.

Now, this doctor did not believe in miracles, I'm sure of that. The reasons why I walked on my feet after just under two weeks without crutches were utterly preposterous to him because his diagnosis is unfaultable. It is still accepted dogma in Mexico that doctors heal the sick. I wondered why there were so many sick people around if doctors do all the healing? Perhaps they kept them sick for experiments or to extend their stay for statistical reasons or want to keep their healing abilities a secret.

In the past China had doctors who got paid a certain percentage from the profits of clients who were healthy and productive. As soon as clients got sick payment stopped, and the doctor did everything in his or her power to restore them back to good health to get paid again once they were back to work. So when did we give up responsibility for our health to doctors who only make money when we are sick, so their interest is not in our well-being but in the money they get when we are ill? Do you think they really want us to be well? They want to make money too, and if people stay healthy doctors here will starve.

Our system is set up in such a clever way as to have insurance in case we get sick, and we pay the insurance premiums and the cost of hospitals beyond what the insurance will cover. We can't even enjoy our vacations because we worry about possible infirmities. Or we don't even go on vacations because of a lack of available money in case it is needed for doctors and pharmaceuticals. We worry ourselves sick over possible hospitalization in another country, and spend fortunes on pills for self-induced anxiety and stress related problems. No wonder the pharmaceutical companies are such a lucrative business. They want to capitalize on your sickness, not your health. They are not selling health; they are selling pills. Let's focus on health and we won't need any pills. Remember: There are million sicknesses but only one health and perhaps that's the reason it's kept secret so healthcare institutions can make money. Did you know that more people live on cancer than dying from it?

Injuries are another issue. Accidents happen and we made some great steps in orthopedics, transplants and other improvements towards longevity and quality of life. But there are also many unnecessary medical procedures like face-lifts, beautifications, and cosmetic surgeries. Too often we allow ourselves to be talked into something that is not necessary, and clever people make a living from this.

Instead of scattering our focus over a multitude of possible sicknesses, let's put our attention on health and realize it is all in the mind. When I decided to walk after a week or two, the healing started. I did not want to lie around and feel sorry for myself or have others shower me with their pity. In fact, I felt happy with the way I recuperated, and the only drawbacks were the screws and the plate that are still bothering me.

I hope my fellow roomies have survived their ordeal and returned to a life of their choice, with the exception of the skeleton that is still dead. And I hope the doctors learned that even old men could show them some new tricks about healing.

Chapter 8

CYNIC?

M OST OF MY life I have observed that differentiating between words and deeds is unique to humans, who seem to be the only species on this planet that do so with diligence. It cannot be the brain that causes this phenomenon because most members of the animal kingdom have brains too, so it has to be something other than that. It's possible that because animals do not speak a human language, and we cannot understand their sounds, we presume they don't make this distinction. Maybe they do differentiate between words and actions, but we will never really know until we learn to decipher their speech.

Let's assume that humans are the only species that have the dubious talent of having words and actions that differ. Why is that? What was the God thinking who presumably gave us this ability? And if we were created in His likeness, would that not imply that He has the same ability? What if He also said one thing and did another? That would put things in a very different light.

Here we have lying, conniving and scheming humans, created by an all-knowing Being, putting shame on their Creator. Or is it possible the proverb "the apple does not fall far from the apple tree" is wrong? What I'm asking may sound heretical, but I have come to the conclusion that I'm free, even to the point of mocking beliefs and

Gods. I think that real freedom is the absence of fear, and not blind devotion to some books that people claim to have been inspired by one of their Gods.

There is no freedom in fear, only slavish obedience. And if there is a God, (and I do mean if), then He or She or It has given man freedom as it presumably has Itself. Therefore I'm free to do as I please, and only need to be aware of cause and effect. The freedom of choice is mine. So God or Gods are above the insults or jokes of humans, and don't need champions to defend them. I think that only insecure humans feel the need to defend their beliefs. This may sound cynical if you consider it is never a god who will punish you; it is always some human who feels insulted.

The Thesaurus describes a cynic as someone who makes a joke of human nature, but this is not my intent.

> *cynical or cynic (adjective)*
>
> *1. doubting or contemptuous of human nature or of the motives, goodness, or sincerity of others*
>
> *2. mocking, scornful, or sneering*
>
> *cynic (noun)*
>
> *1. somebody who believes that human actions are insincere and motivated by self-interest*
>
> *2. somebody sneering and sarcastic*
>
> Encarta World English Dictionary © 1999 Microsoft Corporation. All rights reserved. Developed for Microsoft by Bloomsbury Publishing Plc.

There really is no need to be making jokes of humans because many of them are not capable of understanding a good joke anyway. Humans are doing a good job making themselves the butt of jokes, so I don't have to do that. However, I do like to put a mirror in humanity's face so we can see what it is we're doing. There may be a way out of this labyrinth, but only if we can see where we are. As far as I can see there is no other way except to examine our actions and beliefs, and carefully watch what we say and do. Words that are not the same as deeds are untrue.

I have often found that when things are pointed out that are harmful to growth, inhuman or plain stupid, humans get really upset with the person who points this out, instead of with the conditions. In a country not so far away I discovered an interesting attitude that got me thinking about some fundamental differences between cultures. What I observed was that many public places were equipped with boxes that had inquiry forms about performance and conditions encountered. These forms had been collected and analyzed by a group of people, who then suggested to those responsible what needed to be corrected, and what worked well. To the astonishment of others, and myself the criticism was addressed and improvements made whenever possible. Visitors did not have to be told, "if you don't like what you find go back where you came from."

I would call this an enlightened approach. But when pride of one's heritage or tradition gets in the way, it is amazing how things get out of hand. We don't have to look far to find the clash of heritage and traditions. Such pride is upheld as a high virtue, yet it is the bloodiest thing that exists. Observe the Middle East, North America, Northern Ireland, Asia, and Africa or wherever else you care to look.

Why do we need to have a country, a nationality or religion? Did you ever see a nationality? What is that? Does it make you look different? If you were born in outer space or in the middle of the Pacific what nationality would you have? Would you know it? What can it be used for that we could not do without?

Would you ever encounter a God without anybody first talking to you about it? Did you really hear a God talking to you? Individuals have been sent to mental hospitals for claiming to hear voices, so why is it okay when people claim God is telling them to harm or kill others? Asking questions like this earns you a title or an untimely death, Sir Heretic, Lord Rebel-Rouser or Earl Anarchist. If you ask questions it will open your mind, but may reveal you are in a mental prison imposed by religions, politics and superstition. Each of them is teaching and conditioning the flock to accept their dogmas, which include saying one thing and doing another, i.e. being phony. They claim to be Christians, Moslems, Hindus, Buddhists, Hebrews, to name a few, but as the teachings say, "By their actions shall you know them". Words are cheap and membership easy.

I would very much like to be light-hearted and more relaxed about the things I observe around me, but I see more and more how old folks get robbed and cheated and cleaned out of their life savings. Others are overcharging for services, embezzling money and exploiting their positions. I see corruption in every facet of human behavior, and it makes me wonder about the future of humanity.

If this makes me a cynic then so be it, but I will not stand by and take it with a shrug of my shoulders saying, "Well, this is their culture. I know it's not right and they know it too". No excuses accepted! Would you care to change the trend to indifference in the world, or do nothing and let it be? It starts individually, with each one of us.

Chapter 9

CORRUPTION!

Corruption (noun)

- Dishonest exploitation of power for personal gain

- Extreme immorality or depravity

- The corrupting of something or somebody, or the state of being corrupt

- Immoral or dishonest, especially as shown by the exploitation of a position of power or trust for personal gain

Verb

1. vti to become dishonest, or destroy or compromise somebody's morality or honesty

2. vti to become or cause somebody to become immoral or depraved

Encarta" World English Dictionary © 1999 Microsoft Corporation. All rights reserved. Developed for Microsoft by Bloomsbury Publishing Plc.

W E HAVE COME to think of corruption in association with lesser-developed countries, where it is more blatantly visible than in so-called industrialized countries. But really, what is corruption? In my view it is a deterioration of values and ideals which if present, make life worth living; and when absent, create a state of chaos and unreliability. It is not just exploitation for personal gain and extreme immorality.

To understand the implications of corruption one must look deeper than the symptoms of it. Morality is not the same in all parts of the world, and that which is moral in one place may be immoral in others. A female exposing her thigh in the western world is an everyday occurrence, but watch how this is looked upon in many other countries.

Thomas Moore said it in poetry:

> "Through all the times and all the ages
> All the doctors and the sages
> Two out of fifty scarcely agree
> Of what is true morality."

If my point of view had to be based on morality, I would be very cautious in communicating it to others. I prefer ethics as my guideline. As there seems to be little difference between morality and ethics in common usage, I may have to invent my own definition of ethics to make my point.

I propose to use the word "ethics" to describe a universal conduct that is not about society's religious or political ideology, but rather about unconditional love and acceptance, based on a non-judgmental attitude. For example, a rainy day is a day with rain, not a bad day or a good day. I quite enjoy it after a hot day, when others may not. That's personal preference, and need not be labeled as good or bad. I can say I like it or I don't. It could be seen as immoral to expose oneself to some peoples standards in front of others but not necessarily unethical. It seems we have forgotten how to be neutral and need to take sides. By what standards do we condemn or approve, and see things right or wrong, beautiful or ugly?

We tend to gather people around us who agree with our opinions, and then we create values that others need to accept if they want to join our tribe. If they have their own value system, then we have a conflict. They are wrong and we are right. We create morals for conduct, and start judging those who do not live by these moral standards.

There are a lot of people who do not want to accept all those morals, and because they still want to remain in the tribe for their own particular reasons, they bend the rules or simply break them. That is called corruption. Any breakdown of accepted rules and morals is corruption. Keep in mind: One truth eliminates all lies, and one health cures all diseases.

When we say one thing and do another, it is corruption. When we make promises and do not keep them, it is the same.

Cheating, lying, and deceiving are all forms of corruption because they are dishonesty. While the symptoms are many, the cause is the same. We can take any of the world's problems and when we analyze them they all reduce to greed and fear. And even greed comes from fear. So we resort to corruption out of fear, but hold up the banner of religion or political views (which are also a form of religion) while we rob, murder and exploit. We point fingers at others and do not realize the three other fingers on our hand are pointing back at us.

No wonder Diogenes walked ancient streets with a lit lantern to find one honest person. Out of fear we conform and abandon our principles. We do things we know to be dishonest and then rationalize explanations, creating more lies. This whole world is built on lies and it has been accepted as normal. People who try to remain honest are forced to conform if they want to make some headway. In a world of thieves an honest man is a crook.

I was told today to pay the chief of the justiticia a little money to process a claim. I thought that people got paid to do their job by the government. If the crooks pay them better, will I go to jail? Whose side are they on? As long as people pay bribes they will maintain the system, and are just as corrupt as the one who receives the bribe. I often hear that the government is corrupt. Well, are they not the people who have been elected from their own ranks? How do they expect dishonest people to turn honest when they get into politics?

They don't even know what honesty is. Once in a higher position corruption puts on a face of legality.

This happens all over the world, not only in Latin American countries. It happens in North America, South America, Asia, Africa, Europe etc., but it is easier to see it in others then in our selves. It is corruption when we lie to our children about where they come from, or tell them about Santa Claus. Has that not been realized yet? It is a lie, and we tell them not to lie.

"But those are beautiful lies", people like to say. I heard some beautiful lies that cost someone's livelihood. I'm sure the victims do not much care about the beauty of it. But we are the noble ones. Sure, we like to tell folks how corrupt people are in other countries because it makes us look like the good guys. If you must be a crook at least be honest about it and have integrity. It could have been Jesus of Nazareth who said, "Those who are free of sin shall cast the first stone." Good on ye Mate. Next time beat the moneychangers harder.

Now, how do you get justice when you are living in a place that is run with corruption? If you have an answer to that, please get in touch with me, because at the moment I need to break some bones and laws to get justice. Someone robbed me of a lot of money and I cannot legally get my money back. The police want to get paid before they go to question the guy, but I cannot pay until I get back the money. If I take the law into my own hands, I'm guilty of breaking the law. And to top it all, the police want about as much as was stolen from me.

We are all victims of corruption so let's get ethical. Remember the three fingers. The ripples of change start from the centre and go outward. If we want to change the world, it has to start within, one by one. The world is a big place and we are not big enough to change it, but we can make changes in ourselves. It may take a long time, but it can be done. Don't listen to those who will say, "This is the way the world is." It may be true, but it's the way we made it with our corrupted ways. When we change, the world will change too. Let that thought encourage you.

Patience is a virtue, and if we can learn to practice it and apply it to our world, we will see changes happening little by little in our own small circle of family and friends. With love, patience and perseverance we will succeed. When we make a campfire it starts with a small flame. If we throw a big log on it, it will go out, but use small twigs and branches, blow gently, and it will catch fire easily. Soon we will have a fire going that can light the whole world.

Remember the word love? In today's world it has degraded to a four-letter word that is a synonym for sex, a mere activity without much emotional content. Do you want to make love or go for a walk on the beach? If you walk with me, you show me your love. The other way, you most likely just care about yourself. Sex is an activity often born out of boredom or tension. We don't love out of boredom. The feeling of boredom is in us and we want to get rid of it, so we ask the other to have sex with us. We don't really care about the other. They may be bored too and there is nothing on the TV, so let's get drunk and have sex.

Can you see what I mean by corruption? Values and ideals have been compromised for selfish reasons. I'm glad to see that the younger generation has a new interest in values and ideals as they search for authenticity. If they can cleanse themselves of the old ways that are soiling them, we may have a chance to turn this trend around and create a new world.

Chapter 10

CHARACTERS

WHEREVER YOU GO, there you are.

This statement is enough to create a character that I would travel long and far to meet. Yet I discovered to find characters I only have to look around me. I embarked on this journey to meet them, and to learn of the circumstances that created them.

On occasion I find characters I'm not so sure I wanted to meet. They do make good story material, but there is not much to tell about them. Most likely this is because I did not get to know them well enough to tell their story. They appear to be the kind of folks that are middle of the road; although I'm sure their lives are just as interesting as anybody else's. They just act and behave a way that does not provoke ideas to write about.

Then there are the others. Some are funny, some are dramatic, some are sad. Some make me slap my thigh, double over, and laugh until I need stitches. These last are the folks who make traveling so much of a pleasure that it is nearly impossible to stop! Of course there are others that want me to give up any hope for human kind, but I guess they are needed so we can see how much we enjoyed the former by contrast.

I'm sure there are stories about me also, at least in the form of rumors, gossip, and maybe even the truth; but I have not seen anything in writing yet. Given the nature of most people, it is easier for them to talk about me when I'm not around. In fact, there are stories about me a need to work hard to live up to, most bigger than life. This story is on the characters I observe. To make it easy on them, I will write about me when they're not around.

In the anchorage where I tie up Symbiosis are several boats at anchor a little ways off. Most don't have anybody on board, but a few of them are live-in vessels. The latter are boats occupied by their owners; living beings walking on two legs unless something or someone has forced them to consume unpaid amounts of alcohol, which they swear they will never, ever do again until tomorrow.

One of them has a life size stuffed toy dog that is often more alive looking than his owner, and definitely better behaved than him. Unlike his owner, he never barks at anyone. The dog is passive at least towards other living beings. It doesn't mess the boat, and is not asking for anything.

What I like about this dog is the fact it does not commend god's blessing on people. The dog is well groomed and looks clean as opposed to his owner. I never saw it behaving like a human. Rather it is humane, which is very much the opposite of his owner, the captain. This individual's vessel is an old-timer, a wooden hull boat that has seen better times, with a dock attached to it.

Yes, you read correctly, the dock is attached to the boat, and the boat is at anchor. We get only the boat owner's interpretation of what's legal when asking where the dock came from and it is in contradiction to accepted legal guidelines. However, it serves him as a work platform and for whatever other purpose comes to his mind.

I met him some time back and he greeted me in a gruff way, and then proceeded to chat about his ear that was split in half, back to front, from a fall. He now proudly displays his ear like he is a war hero with a lost leg, back in the olden days where men were men and swords and cannons a way to make money.

He likes to call himself Captain Splitear (Schlitzohr in the German language denotes someone cunning, sneaky and crafty). Nobody calls him that. People talking about him used very noncomplimentary names, and I was curious to see what kind of person he really is. He continued telling me about what he is doing, and asked if there is anything he could do for me because he needed money. Being broke myself I could not use his skills and told him so. He then told God to bless me.

Being suspicious about such folks, I kept contact to a friendly hello, and to the occasional tow of his dinghy when I saw him laboring with oars on windy days. Each time I got a "God bless you" for it. The towing was not a bother, but when he brought up problems and complaints about his friend who drank with him daily until the man fell down, I suggested "Work out your problem with him and not with me. He's your friend; he needs to know what you don't like about him. And if he is your friend and you talk about him in terms that are used for enemies, how do you talk about your enemies?"

His face turned a hue of purple and he cried "Posh you! All of you. I don't need you. I live alone and leave me the #*±! alone. Posh you!" After this earful of curses I stopped offering a tow. A few days later I heard from my mechanic's wife that Captain Splitear was rude and insulting to her husband. He confronted him while drunk, called him names, and in return was told to stay away from the shop or he will be kicked out.

The owner of the shop had assisted Captain Splitear with tools and other things. Now that's gone, so Captain Splitear blames him for undermining his business and keeps "blessing" him. "Shootskees", he said. "I did a lot of work for them and they hate me. Everybody hates me, Posh them all!"

I asked if there is perhaps a possibility that maybe he is the one who hates everybody? I seem to have a knack for making myself the target of mentally deranged and lonely sailors, because his face twisted into an expression as if he unexpectedly bit into a lemon. His eyes were mere slits as he pulled his lips tight over his teeth and snarled, "I don't care! I love everybody. I don't care what they think of me. I live on my boat; I'm Captain Splitear. See this?" And he stuck up a middle finger to demonstrate his love. I was convinced.

A day later he asked me to lend him my generator for two hours so he can do some sanding on his boat. I asked him to bring it back with a full tank, the way he got it. In the evening I went to his boat to save him a rowing trip and to pick up my generator. He was full of gratitude and blessings and we talked for a little while before I returned to my boat with the generator and empty tank.

The following day he asked me to help him find a generator to buy, and I directed him to another sailor who had one for sale. "I don't have the money now, but will have it when I sell my property in Montana" he informed me. "Okay", I said, "When you have the money you can buy it from him".

For a few days I did not see him, and enjoyed the peace of a settled anchorage with a friend. As we prepared Symbiosis for a short sailing stint on the bay he came alongside to tell me that he had bought an older generator, noisier than mine but with more power. He began "blessing" me with four-letter words and waving his hands at me. I would have loved if the hand waving had been with all of the fingers, instead of just one. He then put a healthy distance between my vessel and his dinghy.

Was he worried my laughter would lead to all-out madness and I would hurt him? It was a relief to have him off my back and not have to worry about lending him tools and getting them back empty and dirty. Why wouldn't this make me happy?

The next day while I was answering some emails he came by as if nothing had happened. He reached his hand out for a handshake and was surprised when I asked him what the hell yesterday was all about. At first he pretended he did not remember a thing. Then the amnesia lifted, and he told me I was like all the others who hate him. My surprise was complete.

I thought he liked to borrow things for free, and have people give him jobs and support him with beer and share their fish catch with him, but I stand corrected. Maybe some folks like to be charged, insulted and treated harsh or they don't feel validated?

He continued to blabber his opinion of me and of all the others who are like that, claiming I knew what he was talking about. (I wish!) Then he theatrically dropped on his knees, called me Buddha, raised hands toward the sky, and begged my forgiveness while at the same time cursing me. Passer-by's stopped and wondered if this was perhaps an open-air performance and started digging into their pockets for coins to reward us for the show. Suddenly he remembered that he is Captain Schlitzohr who bends his knees for no one, not even Buddha, jumped to his feet and with a shout, proclaimed that he needs nobody, lives alone, and with a "posh you all" made his exit. Curtains!

The by-standers, stuffed their coins back into their pockets and dispersed slowly. Stunned by the authenticity of this sailor, they even forgot to applaud. That made my day because it reassured me that I'm okay. With a relief I realized how scary it would be to imagine people like this would love me. I think if there were no folks like him, we'd need to invent them. They really bring out the contrast that makes traveling interesting.

Once I watched a soccer game with a great player out-dribbling the other team's players, zigzagging around them, stumbling, getting up, still in possession of the ball then kicking the winning goal into the net, which happened to be his own. Blame dizziness!

This sailor reminded me of that game, and on some days when I'm swamped with things to do that all seem urgent I score like that too, but thank heavens, not every day! Could it be that this Captain Schlitzohr is a very busy man?

Chapter 11

STOOGES

AHH, ANOTHER DAY in Paradise. Where in the world can folks go when they have money? They work hard for 50 weeks in the year saving up money for the long awaited holidays, while planning where they will spend their hard earned cash. Don't worry, because at every destination there are packs of clever people who know how to take care of your hard earned cash. They have spent many years practicing their skills, learned a few words, and speak other languages well enough to get to your wallet. It's done so skillfully that people hand over their money with a smile, then cartwheel to their friends proclaiming the fantastic deal they just made.

Hordes of falsely named tourists, descend year after year from the sky like lemmings from a mountainside to enjoy their transformation into stooges. What are they coming for? What is it that turns normally sane and rational thinking humans into blabbering incoherence, uttering half correctly pronounced words and expecting local folks to understand what they want?

I think the misunderstanding is mutual, but since one wants to buy and the other wants to sell, a deal is made. Money is the greatest translator of all. The more money involved, the better they understand each other. But the more has to be for the vendors. And there are neither limits to what they will ask nor limits to what they will promise.

The stooges are so happy to be on vacations. They don't know the value of the stuff they are buying, and will pay whatever they think it is worth. The sellers just attach a great smile to the junk and some honey sweet compliments, and watch as the female stooges dig into their purses. The male stooges are happy victims for the tanned, doe-eyed female vendors, and smiles and a sly wink seals many deals and even lips and maybe fate, but not wallets.

I thought that tourism had sightseeing, culture exchange, and satisfaction of curiosity about how others live as a motivation, but I stand corrected. To be a tourist is to do with much greater expense and hustle what you could do at home much easier with less cost and without language problems.

And there are other stooges who, like me, come to visit and get trapped with promises and run out of money. Some turn lazy, and some are running from something elsewhere that has not been solved and think changing location will erase the stink they carry on their shoes. There is also the temptation of easier access to illegal substances that feed an unsatisfied need some folks just won't do without. Whatever it is that brought them, they are not safe from con artists.

Those who lived here in Paradise for a while are thought to be immune to the scammers and know all their tricks, but others who are still learning paying the price. It is done like this, "give me a down payment so I can reserve your seat."

This is a good line that works in most cases. Fact is, there are no reservations needed. There are ticket booth selling tickets, and surprise, it is cheaper.

Here is another one, "I need half of the cost to buy the materials or parts". Fact is, if they are in business they will have the parts or can pay for them when they order it and tack it onto your bill. Or you can get the part yourself and give it to them. That way you know what the price is. Otherwise you set yourself up to be screwed big time, as happened to me.

Then there's the "I am an expert" line. These people are lying and mucking up things, but in their minds they really believe in their expertise. However, in know-how and skill I doubt they could repair a bicycle properly. In my experience there are no experts here. I had a mechanic named Pulpo (which means Octopus) come to my boat to do some work on the engine cooling system. He wanted to use slip-joint pliers to remove the bolts. According to him he was the best in the West. The most I expect so-called experts to be able to do is to handle a donkey. It may be different in other parts of the country.

How about this one, "if you buy now, we will give you a good price". It has sucker written all over it, yet it is surprising how well it works.

I love this one, "I will be honest with you".

If they need to emphasize their honesty, beware. Are you really any different than hundreds of stooges before you? They lied to them with the same assurance of being honest. I tell them to keep lying to me because the truth would confuse the hell out of me. I have learned to deal with lies already, so please continue as usual.

Another promises you whatever he thinks you want to hear to get what he wants, but when it is time to deliver or for them to pay up, they disappear like donkeys in dense fog, or come up with reasons why they will not stick to the deal.

And another favorite, "absolutely for sure".

Absolutely for sure it will not happen, is more like it. Unless they get more money out of the deal, there is no guarantee of anything. I have paid for parts to be ordered for an engine on my boat that needed to be repaired and the man spent the money getting drunk and needed more to continue, but not to buy parts.

And finally this, "tomorrow".

You hear it a million times. There is no tomorrow! But we keep falling for it. How many times do we need to have the experience till we get it? Whenever you hear "hey, amigo", be aware. The next line means "how can I screw you today?" whatever else you may hear.

So please tell me, why do we need to go to other places for holidays? Why do we go on vacations and let ourselves get screwed, insulted, cheated and lied to, when we can get the same at home just as good? Is it all for a change of scenery?

Every place I go to I find resorts, golf courses, shopping malls and more hotels then fleas on a dog. Why do we seek to visit pristine virgin places, and find when we leave it was like the place we came from? These places catering to tourism believe visitors came to find the same things they wanted to get away from? I thought we needed to get away from all that same old, same old. Well, I want someone to enlighten me about this human race because I really feel like an alien. Maybe my parents were right after all.

Chapter 12

AGREEMENTS

'M OFTEN RUNNING into trouble with my fellow humans about my ideas and opinions like a mosquito flying head-on into a Mac truck. It usually starts out so promising, "oh, I like the way you think" and "how interesting, I never looked at it that way" and then comes "I don't agree." As if I share my views with others to have them agree or disagree. I'm not looking for converts or followers. I don't want a flock of sheep to look after. I'll leave that to theologians and politicians. Let them be happy caring for the sheep, using their wool, and leading them to the slaughterhouse.

If they need to agree, why don't people just tell me what they want to hear so they can have me tell them what they already know and support their opinions and beliefs? I notice that humans need others to tell them what they want to hear so they can feel safe and secure in their own views and opinions, no matter how stupid or smart. Don't look to me for any kind of support of ideologically infested craziness.

Long ago I found out that I didn't learn anything by listening to others spouting my own views, but for the majority of people this seems to be the normal thing to do. We come up with an idea, or someone plants an idea into our heads, and then we keep playing with it until we believe it is the truth. It then becomes a point of view from which we measure and evaluate other ideas, accepting or dismissing them by agreeing or disagreeing, depending if it fits our point of view or not. I think that only when we listen without agreeing or disagreeing can we learn new things.

Now I am not free of points of views, and when I listen to other people's opinions and I become aware of wanting to agree or disagree I stop and consider why. Invariably I discover it is due to identification with my own ideas and the need to defend or cherish them. Ideas can be made and discarded in a blink of an eye without losing anything of importance, but we are so proud of our "product" that when someone dares to question it we go to war.

I became aware of this odd behavior when I had a conversation with a couple of mixed culture. During our pleasant chat I noticed how tension arose between the couple, and when I asked if there was something the matter, they explained to me that they had a different view about what people need to do to be happy. Then they laid out their ideas. Her idea was not the same as his, and when I asked why love was not sufficient for happiness, and why it was important for one to go along with the other's point of view when all that really mattered was the love they shared, both defended their ideas with teeth and claws.

This couple was very indicative of how the world got to the point of self-destruction over ideas. Love and peace are sacrificed for ideas. Love is a feeling and an attitude of acceptance, and so is peace. It has nothing to do with ideologies or religions. Even an atheist knows love and peace. It's when we mix-up ideas with feelings that ideologies and dogmas create an attitude of who are right, and then all are lost. Love is not an idea, and neither is peace. We fight over who is right, when it is really about what is right.

So it is also when we are on the same playing field. We've all had experiences when we seem to get along just great. We feel one with each other, so much so that we know what the other thinks or is going to say. Then we feel that the other is taking over and hogging the stage, and we are diminishing to virtually nothing. So in order to be noticed we stir up some controversy. Then when our idea is being opposed, we start to defend it because after all it is our "product", and the war is on.

Let ideas be ideas without the need to agree or disagree. See if it works for you. If not, see it for what it is, another view. If it does work you've just learned something new.

There is a view in the world that we need to agree on things to accomplish things, and I can see the value in that for tasks like building bridges and houses and other undertakings, which have a common goal. These are situations when ideas need to be co-coordinated to have the desired result. However the agreement should be restricted to what's necessary to accomplish the task, not to satisfy feelings.

If we need others to make us feel good, insisting they agree with us is a sure sign of fear and of our own incompetence. It would be wise to look for different ideas to learn from, and those ideas are not going to be the kind we already know. Our ideas got us into situations of incompetence and fear in the first place and will not help us get out of them, only deeper into it. So the question is "what are we going to do, other than what we have done so far?"

Someone wisely said, "Doing the same things you've always done will get you the same things you've always got". Therefore we could define ultimate stupidity as doing the same things we've always done, but expecting different results. Pushing takes us to places sometimes, but not through doors marked "pull". By insisting on doing things the way I believed to be the only right way to do it, I have gotten into some really hairy situations.

In my youth I got into fights like most boys, and I learned a few tricks that let me walk away from confrontation victoriously. But in one instance I ran into a guy who previously was beaten by me when I grabbed his wrist and dove under his arm, thus ending up behind him with his arm twisted up on his back. This time he knew what to do. When I grabbed his wrist and dove, he simply turned with me and I ended up looking into his face with both my hands on his wrist. His other hand, in the form of a fist, reshaped my nose. I needed a new technique along with a new nose, and realized there are many ways to skin a cat, but not the same cat.

A suggestion for more peace in the world is this; when we let go of our ideas as an important fact of life and strive for harmony and tolerance instead, the frictions in the world will be lessened, and we begin to promote a better understanding of each other. Agreeing or disagreeing only creates friction that will lead to conflict and argument. That is what we have now in the world today, and it is not advancing peace. So let's focus on Love and Peace, like the idea in the '60s that never carried through the later decades.

When we put our intentions towards harmony and peace in all our dealings with others, and look for a way where no-one walks away feeling like a loser but all feel they have won, then we are on the right track. It is not an easy task but it's doable. What we need is to put more effort into it and examine why we feel a need to be right.

Let's set up a dialogue and listen to each other. Even a terrorist fights to create peace. We may not approve of the method but behind it is the desire to have peace. So what the hell is the problem? That's what we're fighting for too, but fighting can never create peace. It's like fornicating for virginity. Only peace can create peace. Past wars ended because they ran out of resources and people and were too weak to continue, not because they lacked ideas. And wars have always been about ideas. One group did not agree with another. Look into any family conflict, what are the reasons for arguing? Ideas that one person has and others do not. When people put their efforts into solving a situation, all of sudden things go smoothly. That is called agreement for a common goal, and it has nothing to do with common feelings.

I once had to tell an employer to tell me what to do, not how to do it. What mattered was the end result, not the method, but the fool was insisting that I should do it the way he did the job, even though my way was better and easier than his way. He told me that he did it his way for more than twenty years and if it were good for him, it would be good for me too. I replied that his forefathers dragged their knuckles in the dust, and I wanted to know if he was doing that also.

It seems to me that people only feel secure when others follow their lead, and maybe feel their leadership is threatened when people find other ways. Perhaps they think that when people see different approaches they will turn away and abandon the leader, so instead of adapting new ways, those in leadership roles try to force their methods on the group. They want us to agree with their ways so they can feel secure.

That's how traditions are created, and it is one of the most regressive ways to keep people in line. Isn't it funny how well it works? When someone mentions tradition almost everybody pays reverence, and nobody dares to question its validity. We abandon common sense and good judgment in favor of tradition. We agree to stupid things because it is a tradition.

It's time to wake up from Zombie-ism and question tradition, established procedures, and customs. Let's start fresh and ask why it is important to follow someone's lead and ideas.

Sometimes there are necessary reasons to come together under one leader for a given task, but once the task is finished we need to be individuals again. Stay away from habits, they only create a rut and it takes a lot of effort to get out of them. Have the courage to be you; it is impossible to be somebody else.

Chapter 13

HEATSTROKE

A LOT OF THINGS can happen in a day, and when the sun goes down. It goes down every day and then it comes back, but on the other side, the opposite of the side where it went down. You can record your daily observations. When you examine them some time later, it may seem like a parade of incredible happenings that appear to be products of fantasy when you tell them, yet they are true. Others before me noticed this phenomenon and wrote scientific papers about it and became famous. Some were ordered to rescind their heretical views or burn on the stake. There were a lot of things (and people) at stake in those days.

But it is not so far from those days in southern latitudes where there are lots of old habits. Superstition and ignorance combined with traditional customs keep those old days alive. Some readers may have heard of Puerto Vallarta. It is situated in a beautiful (at least when viewed from the distance) Bay southeast of Cabot St. Luca. That particular day in Puerto Vallarta the sun penetrated this tradition soaked place in spite of the dark traditions still adhered to by many. I'm sure about this because I could read papers and see people without using a lamp. The sunlight affected some of them strangely. It could also be possible that what I experienced that day was an accumulation of exposure to sun that was too long for the brain to tolerate without showing some bizarre side effects.

If you've heard of re-fried beans, sun-dried tomatoes and suntan, I'm sure you've heard about sunstroke. Sunstroke has been blamed for many mysterious actions. We have learned to accept the symptoms of it and have even found some treatment for it. Sun-fried brain is a new word and illness and no cure has been found yet. No, it's not a delicacy, unless you are into really weird food. For the life of me I cannot explain some apparently human action that defies a reasonable explanation, even if sunstroke was the cause of it. Just take "Celebra fritta del sol" as a new human disease, and learn to live with its effects. It may even give you a laugh, as it did me.

Now, let me stand back a little to give you a better view. That particular day started with a predicament. The engine on my boat was awaiting repairs and I needed to take my batteries to another boat to charge them if I wanted to read a book on cloudy days in the cabin. The 12-volt batteries were down to a scant 10.5 volts, and I have no shore power available here at anchor. When I got to the other boat a fellow was there. His name shall remain anonymous to protect the guilty. I told him of my intention to charge the batteries, and also that I would need a voltmeter to measure how much they charged.

He just happened to have one that he wanted to sell for a hundred Pesos to buy beer. I had no money at hand but told him I could get it by tomorrow and asked him if there was a chance I could borrow it to check the batteries. "Okay" he said, "but we need to go to the bar where this apparatus is. I can have credit till tomorrow". We went to the bar. I got the meter and took it to the boat to see how the batteries were doing. Then I returned to the bar where this man was by now talking to a Canadian guy who in the past had sailed on the boat where the batteries were percolating.

I knew him and said hello. Then I told Mac (fictitious name) that I would buy the meter from him. We agreed to the payment the next day, because the boat would need one anyway. Then this Canadian guy jumped in and asked Mac how much he wanted. He told him what he told me, a hundred pesos. This fellow pulls a hundred from his wallet and hands it to Mac. Then he asked me to give him the thing and when he got it, walked to the water's edge and hurled it into the water.

The first thing that entered my mind was to ask him what was the purpose of that, or how much did he drink, or what was he smoking? Those are questions you can ask a half-intelligent person and you may get a half-intelligent answer, but what can you ask someone who only pretends to be half-intelligent? I was seriously considering asking his partner how she got him to speak and walk upright. In the past I have had no reason to suspect that the human species harbored this kind of behavior, so the only explanation left to me is to assume that the sun is behind it, just like it is today, behind the clouds. It may also be the local drink called Tequila that got to him. Regardless of the cause I made sure to put some distance between him and me just in case it was contagious.

There are many instances like this when I do a double take on what I see, because it does not fit into my concept of intelligent behavior. As hard as I try to understand these actions, they defy any explanation. The funniest thing is when I hear them talking about other people who do the same things, they find it just as nuts as I do. Isn't that the pot calling the kettle black?

After this episode I decided to try a little craziness on my own to see how it would come across to others. It was possible that I would either be accepted as normal, or that I would get a strange look. It went like this. I had offered sailing lessons and assistance to restore a yacht in exchange for a dinghy with motor. The dinghy had been assigned to me, and was to become mine after it got fixed. However it was then promised to someone else as payment for some work he had done, and then again to someone else who also did something that needed to be paid for. So there was this dinghy, mine by right because I had done the work I was asked to do, that was being used as payment to three different people.

The idea is as old as humanity; promise several people the same thing as payment, and when it comes time to collect the debt, let the creditors fight it out over who has the ownership of it. Okay, that may have worked in the Dark Ages, but I mistakenly assumed that they were done with. So I told the man with whom I had the deal that the boat was promised to me for my work, and therefore it could not be given to someone else. I was assured that indeed the dinghy was mine, so I took it.

Oh what a fracas that caused! One fellow accused me of stealing his boat. Another threatened me with the police. And a third accused me of causing him to be homeless. In the middle of all this were my views of what is just and fair. I forgot I was in Mexico. Normally I would accept customs if they are uniformly practiced in a region, but when it comes down to "I can do this to you but you cannot do it to me", I get a bit annoyed. In this case it was not even that. It was blatant fraud and Gringos did it. Not surprisingly that is why the fraudsters come, because they can get away with it here.

There are no uniform laws in this state, even if they talk about it as if there were. I asked the police to help me with a recovery of 7000 pesos that a guy posing as a mechanic embezzled from me, and the policeman asked me for 2000 pesos to do his job. I would love Mexico if I weren't so straight. Of course, it may not be this way everywhere, and I want to beg pardon of all the honest people here if I hurt their feelings, but I still want to find just one person that I can trust unconditionally.

I wonder if perhaps I expect too much, and want to have a perfect world where all is honest and reliable. But I also find that I can live with thieves and even murderers as long as they are without pretense. What's a murder among friends here and there? Still better than wholesale killing in some desert country for oil, while pretending to be doing it for peace and liberty. Liars, on the other hand, get my goat. I don't mean lies for entertainment purposes. A fellow who had been tied to a wheelchair from birth on and claimed to have been a test pilot and a secret agent once had me in stitches with his stories and I loved every minute of it. He knew and I knew, and we accepted each other completely. Yet, when it is done to gain your trust and then take advantage, it is as low as I imagine anyone can sink.

Unfortunately this is what I see here. At least in Puerto Vallarta I have seen too many cases just like that. It saddens me to think that I may be including some who do not deserve harsh judgment. But when I hear others having bad experiences and see how they have been treated, I cannot help thinking that it may be better to change plans. Instead of coming here, go to see other parts of the world that do not have this kind of attitude towards visitors. Someone told me that we cannot change people and I understand that, but when we start spending our money somewhere else and get better treatment, that will make them want to change on their own.

Going to places where no tourists have gone may be the answer. Tourists have a bad habit of wanting the comforts of home and the newness of a holiday destination. Forget it! Holiday is to get away from the same old, and to have something new to experience and talk about. How new can it be to play golf in Mexico, to get drunk in Australia, or to get high in Thailand?

When we start to wake up and look at the value our money gets, how the price relates to the effort put into creating a product, and what locals would pay for it, we will have a better understanding. Then cheating and exploiting us will become harder, and honest business will have a chance to prosper. It would benefit everyone. As long as we remain ignorant and pay what we think something is worth to us, we will be exploited, and crooks will rule.

There is something to be said about social responsibility, and it means that we need to be aware what our payment of inflated prices will do. It will allow the rich to become richer while the less fortunate will suffer. The rich can afford the inflated prices and in the end they will control the market and dictate prices. Here in Puerto Vallarta I see what happens when we pay big prices. The tourists pay the prices that are asked. After all they are in a holiday resort, and high prices are to be expected. But locals cannot afford it here, so they have to move or make more money.

Where can they get money? From the tourists. How? By raising the prices on their goods. They know it is not worth the price because it does not cost much to make, but they need the money to be able to live in the area. This creates a dishonest attitude. It is not far from being a liar, a thief, and maybe even worse. Since the time I arrived here I have observed and listened to many opinions and complaints about what is going on in Puerto Vallarta. Some people love it here and keep coming back year after year, so they must be finding something that is suiting them, or else they have a thicker skin or wallets than others.

Friends of mine coming from Switzerland, France, Netherlands, Canada and other far away places and living here for more than twenty years have not much good to say about the attitudes of the locals. The thievery, dishonesty, unreliability and stupid pride is holding them back from higher education and a better understanding and better life. This country has more potential to be a First World country than many others, and the only thing that prevents it is pride, traditions, ignorance and the indifference to basic principles of ethics.

So why are we here? There are some that came to escape a high-pressure society, others to escape the Law, and some are seeking warmer climates or economic reasons. I'm sure there are as many reasons as people, and they all want a better life, but the gods put effort before benefits. If we want to ski down a mountain slope, we first must climb the mountain. Dishonesty may bring us rapid profit, but in the long run word gets around and the customers stay away. Word of an honest deal also gets around, and will attract clients for the long term.

The locals have had their share of corruption and violence, and coping with it in the same manner was a way of living for a long time. So it is important to raise awareness about these conditions and not just accept them as a cultural thing. Only crooks feel at home in a corrupt situation. The ethically aware people who want change are the outcasts. In a land of thieves and liars, an honest man is a crook.

I see many people wearing a cross around their neck and in other forms of jewelry, the sign of devotion and of Christianity. The biggest crooks have the biggest crosses of gold displayed, and "God bless you" on their lips, all to butter us up and gain our trust. I've been banned from places because I do not think and speak like them. My words offended the "good Christians" whose teachings from their Bible include tolerance, yet they are the ones who tell others not to allow me in their establishments or they will not come anymore. They were the first to condemn the Moslem outrage at the pope's words (Oct. 2006) and demanded tolerance because "it was just words" that were quoted by him.

In fact I don't preach any religion and have no answers, but I ask a lot of hard questions and point out contradictions in actions and words, and that seems to create quite the unrest among the Establishment.

I don't see any difference in their Christian behavior from that of the Moslem world when they hear something that they don't like. We can say whatever it is we want to say, but it better be what they want to hear, or else! I say that if the Gods take offence, let them punish the offender. A lightning bolt from a clear sky would do. That could be considered proof of their existence. But I only see people getting offended.

The more we claim to be Christian, Buddhist, Jewish or any other religion and the more we want to convince others of our honesty, the more the opposite is true. Honest people do not proclaim their honesty, they live it, authentically. I'd like to emphasize that people are more authentic when they are angry than when friendly. There are not a lot of authentic, real people around, but there are a lot of conformists who try to please everybody to go ahead in life, and to fit in. Why is it if I resist their attempts to make me accept the same beliefs they have, that I'm the one causing the problem?

Ah, conformity is valued as highly as gold! When we heel like well-trained dogs we are accepted and climb in the hierarchy, but be a freethinker and we get nailed to the cross. We accept hypocrites, liars, and other dark, shady characters, but fear and reject those who point them out. Our greatest teachers and spiritual guides have been persecuted and even killed, as happened to Socrates, Jesus, Gandhi, Bhagwan Rashnish and Martin Luther King. Even Lao Tzu, Buddha and Krishna and many others had to watch their backs. What does that say about us? These people never hurt anyone. In fact they did the opposite by trying to help and guide humanity to a more aware state. Go figure!

People are angry with the person who points out the crap. They are not angry with the fact of the crap, or with the one who created it. We are so bent on dishing out guilt, perhaps to feel better about ourselves, that the fact of the crap remains unsolved. How are we ever to grow up if we keep on doing what we have always done? Pointing fingers at others produces three pointing back at us, and that could help us become aware of our own stuff. But we focus more on the one finger and overlook the others.

Changes in the world come about when we change first. It is not in our power to change others, so we might as well start with us becoming role models. Nature gives us plenty of examples that all start within, like dropping a pebble into water. The rings start from the centre going outward and affecting all that the ripples touch. Be aware what those ripples may cause, and you will be one step closer to Tao.

Chapter 14

PASSPORT CHA-CHA

BUREAUCRATS! WE CAN'T live with them and we can't shoot them. That would be against the laws that the bureaucrats made and we are all bound by. So what is the solution? Just recently I had to get my passport renewed and experienced how the bureaucratic system is doing it's work by not doing it.

I have always been told that the people we vote for to represent us in government are civil servants, meaning they serve us. Surprise! It's no secret that this is not the case, but the new rule has got to be the stupidest thing I have ever had to deal with for a passport renewal.

My passport from my beloved country of Canada was issued in 2001 and was good for a year, unless extended to 2006, which I had done in Mexico. The document expired on my birthday, and now in 2007 had been in a dormant state for almost a year. At the consulate I found out that if I had not come in before my birthday I would have needed more documents with new photos to prove who I am. As if I would change in a year plus a day so dramatically!

Once I was asked in a bank to identify myself in order to cash a cheque, and seeing my mirror image in a window I was able to identify myself without a problem and so got my money. Those were the good old days.

So here I am at the consulate listening to this news from a lovely young lady behind the counter.

First of all, I cannot have my old passport extended anymore, I need to have a new one that is improved and guaranteed to keep terrorists from getting them. Aha I think; this is a good idea if people are honest and stick to the rules. But we all know terrorists are not. Bureaucrats make things so impossibly difficult that honest people need to become dishonest to get things done.

I have lived in Mexico now over five years, and I am a bit familiar with the Mexican ways. Money is power, but I did not expect to find this happening in a Canadian consulate in the form of new rules. The new fees are now $75. They used to be just $20 a little more than 5 years ago. Also it will take 4-6 weeks before I get the new passport. Why so long? If we are looking for a criminal we can have a positive ID in minutes. Why not use the old passport, extend it if the picture still is current enough, and phase it out over time with new ones.

We could save a lot of money, time and line-ups at the passport office and terrorists would have a hard time knowing when and which passports to use since they don't have the data the offices have.

When you get better service, you expect to pay more, but when you are getting lousy service, why should it cost more? To top it off, I do all the work. I need to have new photos in another place and pay big bucks for two 1 ½" X 2" color prints, signed and stamped on the back and testifying that indeed the picture is a true likeness of me, just in case someone might take a photo of me showing the face of someone else. Then I have to find a guarantor who is either a lawyer, doctor, signing banker, politician or a similar dark and shady character from the movie "The Godfather" to state that they have known me for at least two years.

I made a point to stay away from those characters when I found out what they do. Doctors kill, lawyers lie, politicians are corrupt, and bankers rob you blind. Why are these the people we should trust? Are these the new role models of our times? We are deeper in it then I thought. Remember, it is bureaucrats who send us to them. They trust them to do what, I wonder?

Can this lovely and intelligent young lady not compare a picture with my face and certify it is of me? If she is not trustworthy enough to tell the truth what is she doing in the consulate? I think she deserves our trust to make decisions in matters about passports. Just run the information through a computer and in seconds she will know if there is a problem and take it from there.

Now I must take the passport to a courier service and pay another high price to deliver it to the embassy and have it returned to the consulate for me to pick up again. Consulates have their own mail services much more trustworthy and secure than private companies, so it makes me think there might be some political agenda behind this new rule, perhaps to stuff someone's pockets. I would like to see Canadians lead by wise and intelligent example in this crazy world, and not contribute to the problem with more stupidities. We have enough already, and jumping on the bandwagon of "You are with us or you are against us" politics is not only foolish, it is outright dangerous.

Chapter 15

STUPOR

A s MUCH AS people like to talk about holidays, being in a place in the sun where they relax and drink Margaritas, the holiday experience is marred not only by pushy street hustlers and relentless vendors, but by pesky insects of all kinds. Admit it. You want to squash them, hit them, shoot them, poison them, drown them and in short, terminate them! I'm not sure who you are thinking about as you read this, but for now let's stay with bugs, the kind that are using more than two legs and wings to get around.

We find them in the jungle and on the streets, but mainly it is our rooms that seem to have an irresistible attraction for them, and also our dishes loaded with yummy food. Sometimes I wonder how many insects per spoonful I get to consume during a meal. At night they are the talk of the town. Movie stars can only hope to be talked about as much. We humans are also very popular with the bugs, as we can testify in the morning in front of the mirror after a night on the town with the obligatory consumption of several beers and a bottle of tequila.

When nature's call is becoming hard to ignore in the middle of the night and staying in bed is not really an option, we wake up fully from our half-sleep en route to the bathroom to the sound of a too slow cockroach crunching underfoot. Returning to our bed, we fight off Mexican kamikaze mosquito squads until we fall into an exhausted sleep. No wonder some people can't recognize themselves in the mirror, and look for a familiar face that could possibly identify them.

Our repertoire to control this insect plague has been limited to swatting and waving along with some commercially available means to keep them at bay. There have been many inventions and strategies for combating the insect population. We have tried insecticides, repellents, lights, zappers, chemicals, acids and even basic hand to hand, mano a mano, strategies, but the odds continue to favor the marauders.

They come en masse in all sizes, forms and shapes. They invade our habitat and shamelessly pillage our food supplies and extract huge quantities of our lifeblood. They leave behind itchy bumps, welts, blisters and a mounting desire in their victims to take revenge. For peace loving and life respecting beings this is a great challenge, and even though we may believe that eventually the life force will return (hopefully in more benign form), it is with heavy heart that we conduct our killing. (We all know this is a lie of course.)

In our search for effective measures we have come up with several deadly ways to get rid of the invaders. And when even one of these enemies is vanquished we have a devilish delight over our success. We make jokes about the way it got squashed, electrocuted, or poisoned, before or after it had breakfast. "Oh look, this one tried to get away with your blood. And see how flat she is now? Quick! Wash the blood off your hands so they will not have evidence against you in a Court of Law." How about "this one is so ugly now that even her mother will not want her back." And then there's "Wow! Nice and crispy. Want a taste?" Others get mashed so bad even God would have trouble reassembling them.

When we are lucky enough to spray them, we remain close to the legs-up-and-kicking, spinning, and doing the Pilates workout exercises infected bug, risking our own health from the poison gas just to see our adversary meet it's Maker. Due to concerns for our health, we came across a new method of eliminating our adversary. Booze! Yes, you read right. Booze as in alcohol. We went to a

Drugstore and bought a bottle of 90% pure alcohol, filled a spray bottle with it, and lay in ambush for our assailants.

It's just like in some bars Down Town where the girls in their sexy outfits lie in wait for a suitable and unsuspecting tourist. They rush the mark and shoot and shoot and shoot Tequila down his throat while blowing a whistle. The victim does seem to like this as he staggers away with a euphoric grin on his face singing a Mariachi tune, "Ay-yay-a-yay," at the top of his lungs. We think this is great.

So let's throw a party and invite all the annoying insects for free booze. When they are sloshed we can watch them die of alcohol poisoning. It will literally be a killer party. The few who survive will have a hangover that will last them for the rest of their life. And what's more, they all die happy, possibly with a song and a grin on their face or whatever you may call that frontal part of their head. But for sure they will have a more pleasant passing then before. We hope word gets around and we will be host to many of their kind. The human bugs are not invited, the expenses due to their resilience would be staggering. We will have to think of something else to do with them.

Chapter 16

VIRILITY

WHAT SHAME VIRILITY is wasted in our youth. By the time we know what to do to make best use of it, it's gone, like an April shower. Young people have so much of it that they go around and twitch all day wanting to get some action. When they succeed it is over in such a short time, they hardly noticed it had begun.

On the other hand, when old folks start the game their interest has faded into other areas, like remembering that the stove is still cooking the remains of an unfortunate casserole meant to be a dinner surprise. It all started so well. The champagne is still in the bucket, but the ice is gone, and the water would make the bunch of roses happy. Gone is the memory of the sweet words, the special attention to details in her dress, and the plan for the evening. When we start the game again, a kind of silliness takes hold and we make good fools of ourselves. Mushrooms taste better fresh than re-heated.

We all know how to flirt. In fact, age perfects us, and our charm and honesty are our best sides. There are no problems as long as flirting is just that, but when flirting catches fire we are in hell's kitchen. And there is the issue of age. Most men love young women in full bloom, and when we are lucky and get a positive response to our advances we drop twenty years in age. The lackluster eyes and the tired gait are gone, who was that man who had arthritis just yesterday?

I'm reminded how it's been said "man has good sex for twenty years, then becomes a stud horsing around for another five, followed by five more monkeying, and finally makes a jackass of himself till he dies". Talk about a metamorphosis.

Yet our lady friend is glowing with our compliments. Having the attention of an older, distinguished gentleman is a special honor because it makes her feel more mature. And the prospect of being treated like a lady is better than with young men, who only have one thing on their mind.

Make no mistake, older men have the same thing on their minds, but know how to cover it up with finesse. Ladies also have the same thing in mind, but they want to make others believe they don't. Why else do they display their goods and go out with a man who issues an invitation? In the end all roads lead to Rome.

There is nothing wrong with it. We are sexual beings whose biological function is unlike many animals that come into heat only during certain peak times of the year. So forget political and religious reasoning and artificial moral codes, and embrace your true human nature without pretensions.

The saddest situation is when we treat and deal with our desires like an object for sale or for bargaining. Is it not degrading when we pay money for women to share their affections with us? A woman accepting money for sex must feel like a victim. She does us a favor and sacrifices herself and her body for money. Can we not get intimacy because we are so ugly that we need to pay for it? Where is our self-worth? Can we not imagine that women enjoy our affections too, and if we are really good are we not worthy to be paid also, or at least call it even? Consider this: Sex without love is either rape or business, also called prostitution.

If we both want love, let's have it. Strange how men think they can go around and feel like a "real" man when having "scored" with a number of women, but women are labeled anything else when doing the same thing. Why aren't they called "real" women? We encourage boys to go out and get'em, have fun and afterwards we approvingly smile and say: thata-boy. A woman can turn into a whore in the instant when she stops having sex with *you*.

Sex is not bad but what we make of it is. We don't see it as an expression of affection or love, but as bond that imprisons the other so that they become our property. We then think we have rights instead of privileges. It is an honor when we are intimate with another because we share affection with that person. It does not make that person our property. The experience is ours and nobody can take that from us, but the person is free to go whenever they decide. Love is an experience, not a thing that can be had. It changes like day to night. Breathing is not only taking a breath in. It must also go out, or it would not be complete.

Hanging on to another will make them want to leave. Nobody wants to live in a cage unless they are afraid to be free. The fear of freedom is due to a lack of self-confidence, of being afraid what others will think of us. When we live by other people's expectations we are their powerless slaves. A free person is not afraid. When fear comes into our lives we begin to conform and lose our dreams, our love, and our joy of life.

Young people have been deceived with the idea that when they have sex with someone, they also have rights and responsibility along with it. Out of duty, guilt, or obligation they enter into a commitment that often ends in a bad relationship. Then they look for ways to get what they want outside of the relationship, which in turn creates more guilt, lies, deception and a falseness of being. I have been accused to promote free sex but the way I see it, the alternative is paying for it in some form. Is that not called prostitution? What happened to: I please you, you please me?

When we get older we understand that we are not doing the honest thing, but it is difficult to get out of the rut we are in. Also there are friends, perhaps children, parents, and mother and father in-law to consider. So the majority of the human population pretend all is well, and continue living a lie. If you want to be different you will make yourself a target of ridicule, and at best become an outcast. Or they will hate you for lecturing them to make yourself special and better than them. You will not be invited to parties. Even friends start avoiding you. Word will get around that you are a strange guy and no fun to be with. The price you pay for wanting to be a better person by being honest is very high indeed. People prefer hearing a lie to an inconvenient truth.

At least youth are not interested in all this heavy stuff, and sow their seeds without much thought. All would be well if they did not have stupid ideas planted into their heads already, and when the surge of the hormones subsides they remember these ideologies again. Then slogans like "do as I tell you, not as I do" get created.

Too bad, wisdom comes with age, because it would be better having it while young. There are too many of us old folks who are giving good advice because we cannot continue being a bad example no matter how hard we try. I still remember when I thought it was desirable to be able to perform five times in one day. Now I'm glad to perform once a year, with the expectation I'll be remembered for five years. Believing that takes the sting out of advancing age. Others mistakenly think we are losing hair, when in reality we are gaining face. We oldsters can excuse our failures due to our age, but what excuse do young folks have; business pressures, performance anxiety, "sorry, but I'm gay?"

A Woman can always claim to have the infamous headache, but what about a man? We need to invent something to be pardoned, because only wimps use the "I'm tired and exhausted" routine, and there will be a snowball fight in hell before we would admit to being wimps. But advancing age is accepted and even seen by some ladies as a challenge to make it all better by proving they have magical powers. And they do.

It was amazing how an elderly gentleman, who was with a much younger companion he introduced as his niece, shook off a knockout blow from the sailboat's boom. A ram would have crumbled to his knees, but this old goat just said "oops, gotta watch that" and continued telling her how he shopped heroically alone in Bangkok and single-handed stopped four potential cutthroats by handing over his wallet with $1000 in it. The wide-eyed, open-mouthed admiration of his niece was magical. He was her hero, and the six-course dinner was paid for without the blink of an eye. The swelling of his head must have impressed her immensely, because throughout the evening she hung on his lips like a leech. Some nieces are more magical then others.

Every now and then I experience miracles that can only be explained by the presence of the fairer sex. It surprises me how often men who are rude and boisterous turn into gentlemen when a lady is present. They are courteous and lay off the four-letter words in conversations. Other men turn timid and display an attitude of helplessness, and others become show-offs. All these changes in behavior are done to fulfill their potential by impressing and attracting the chosen object of their affection. It is the result of hormones in action.

Since I am a man, I cannot imagine how women feel about such displays of mating ritual, but I would love to hear some comments from the female population. How do women react to male advances, and what do they consider to be effective? I often hear that they like it when men are real, but I have yet to see a man being real in the presence of women. We men seem to carry so many optional roles with us; it would take an onion thousands of years to grow that many layers.

And what about women? What do they do to attract men? To me it seems the first thing they are concerned about is their looks. Inner beauty is second or even third on their list of concerns. They know men well enough to realize what a man sees first, namely; bust, waist, butt, legs, face and hair, not necessarily in this order. Looks are important for women to be attractive, and they know it.

Men seldom ask for intelligence in women and often find it intimidating, because it dims their own imagined intelligence. Why she needs a man if she is intelligent is a fair question. So women do not display their smarts until the man is caught in the Venus trap. Now, that's using intelligence.

Men are so easily lured. All that is needed is a display of some of the goods with an encouraging smile, and men will follow women almost anywhere and do almost anything to convince them of their worthiness. They fly to Mars to astonish the world, and to demonstrate their prowess to the females. As the saying goes, "behind every successful man is a woman who put him there".

So we can see that nature has provided us with the sexual incentive to accomplish things that we normally would not do. Let's acknowledge this power and not put it in a political straight jacket. A thing I learned in the southern latitudes is that when you look at a woman appraisingly, they actually smile at you for noticing them as a woman, while in our northern parts they sue you for sexual harassment.

Face it folks, sex is a reality that will not go away, and political correctness only perverts it. In fact, if it weren't for sex we would have gone the way of the dinosaurs long ago. I love looking at women, and will not avert my gaze when I notice a good-looking girl or woman like many men do when meeting her eye. It is part of the ritual to look and notice.

A woman dressed in a very masculine way, including a tie, once harangued me for sexual molestation because I looked at her ample bosom, although I had not said a word or made an offensive gesture. If she hated men, why was she dressing like one? From suppression springs perversion, does that ring a bell? Remember the outcry of society when sexual molestations in Ireland, Canada, United States and Europe committed by Christian Brothers came into the light and then quickly hush-hushed? Heaven knows we've had a lot of examples. Let's go with the flow, shall we?

Chapter 17

MEXICAN HAT DANCE

MEXICO HAS INVITED the world to visit, and the world has responded with throngs of visitors to its sunny shores and tradition soaked customs. The fun and endless parties make it hard to think that there may be some things that are not what they seem.

It's possible that flirting and getting VD is more fun in Mexico, and that getting drunk may be cheaper than at home. After the first few layers of sun burned skin are peeled off, even the tours are exciting. But beneath this happy facade of activity is a sad reality that tourists seldom see during their short stay, and may not even want to know about.

You arrive at the airport, gather your bags, and the music begins. Salsa or mariachi music will sound in your ears and vibrate in your skull until your body begins to twitch and you break into a kind of gait that some people call dancing. And why not? You came for holidays, to relax, to party, and to get a tan that your co-workers will envy and will let the world know that you were on vacation in some sunny country.

People smile and welcome you to Mexico. They call you Amigo, which translated means "Sucker" and behave like they have been waiting specially for you. They will call you over as if they have been assigned to you personally to take care of you and make your stay one to remember, and remember you will and you would do well to keep away from them.

Walking down the street you will be hustled endlessly to go to a Timeshare presentation, and with promises of a "better deal". On the beach you get the same hustle, and every minute someone wants to sell you something. You learn to say, "No thank you" in Spanish, but they do not understand your refusal. You will go home in need of a vacation from your vacation. Welcome to Mexico! The fact is you are not welcome at all; it is your money that is welcomed. The more money you bring and spend, the more you will appear to be welcome.

Mexico's wealth is not derived as much from its exported goods or products as it is from the income, which the tourist industry provides. There's nothing wrong with this, and many foreigners make a decent living in Mexico also, but unfortunately ethical standards are lacking.

The people calling you Amigo don't know you from a brick in the wall, and all they want is your money. What they offer in return is an inconvenience and a necessary expense for them to get your big bucks, and then you better go home. Tourists are seen as moneybags. The names you are called, sometimes to your face, are not the kind you want to brag about. You will be cheated, robbed, taken advantage off, insulted, and told to leave if you don't like it.

In defense of some locals I must say that not all of them would do that to you. There are some authentic and legitimate vendors, who can be identified by a sign saying NO TIME SHARE. And there are a lot of others who resisted the temptation to become dishonest but you will not meet them often because they live a quiet and unobtrusive life under the rubble. You will meet them when you get to mingle with the common people away from the highly visible crowd.

However you need to be careful with these people too. The temptation to make more money off of you than is fair is always present, so comparing services and prices is a good idea.

Be wary of the words "a better deal". They are always connected with a Timeshare presentation where the loser is going to be you, unless you are willing to spend a lot of money.

If you come to Mexico with your own car, bike or boat, make sure your vehicle is in good order. There is no quality service, no professionalism, no guarantee, and no parts available for the majority of vehicles. Craftsmanship is so poor that a first year apprentice in the northern countries could be considered a specialist here. Reliability is non-existent, and integrity of workers is nil. Your vehicle will be mexicanized, which means jury-rigged in boater's language.

If you are lucky repairs may work for a while, but the price you pay is much higher than you would pay at home. They often demand payment before the job is done. They say it is "for parts" and then disappear with your money. If you ask for your money back, they tell you they don't have it. That you can believe because it was spent to cause the next day's hangover, and the job is still not done, plus they now need more money, often to cure their hang-over with more beer.

They will take advantage of your needs and laugh at you for being gullible. They will rob you and when you go after your money, they will threaten you with a lawyer for harassment. This is not a joke. It has really happened and not only once. One incident that is a disgrace to mankind involved stealing from senior citizens. A purse was snatched with a substantial amount of money that was to be used as payment for a doctor's fee.

The purse contained important papers besides the cash and credit cards, and two cell phones. A few days later the victim made a call to her stolen phone and someone answered. It turned out this person bought it from the thief. He pointed a finger at the thief who naturally denied the theft, but claimed he knew who did it. Of course he knows; he sees him whenever he looks in a mirror!

All this lady wanted was to get her papers back. She was willing to let this fellow get away with everything else without legal prosecution, because of the hassle involved. While this is understandable, it will only encourage thieving to continue. Still worse is the attitude of the authorities. They ask you for money to recover your property.

They might as well steal it themselves. Why bother sharing it with a thief?

Then there are the so-called tradesmen, the mechanics, electricians, shipwrights, painters and fiberglass applicators etc. You will be hard pressed to name a handful that know what they are doing in all of Vallarta. Even those tradesmen from the United States and other places now resident in Mexico are not worth the money they ask. The locals claim to be a specialist in whatever you need to have done, but a chimp would do a better job without having any training at all.

Some shops have high-tech analysis computers where the results of a test are displayed on a screen, but the fellow operating it has a hard time reading in his own language let alone in English. Yet nobody questions how this guy would be able to understand what the problem is. A well-known European brand car dealership has some car salesmen who speak English, but none of the technicians do.

In the marina in Puerto Vallarta there are many guys claiming to be specialists of some sort, and so they may be, but in exactly what you will only find out several months later when your money is gone, and you are still waiting for the work to be done. Many boaters have left their boats and money here for some work to be done while they were away. When they returned they found nothing done and the money gone. They then had to do the job themselves and pay more money to the boatyard for the additional time needed.

In some cases when a job is done it has just made the original problem worse than it was before, and they will not take responsibility for the bad workmanship. You will have to pay for the new parts they installed, and now you will also need a specialist flown in from the States to remedy the damage they caused, all paid out of your pocket.

Maybe your engine will be "repaired" by a "mechanic" named Ninja over a period of a few months, while you are being asked for more and more money, and after a short time the engine will cease and it will be the fault of anybody but the "repairman".

They cannot be held accountable because there is no governing body to regulate these "mechanics". There are no knowledgeable people here with any authority that could implement an ethical code of standards for work done. That's why it is called Wild Mexico.

There is a strange mentality in Mexico that is very disturbing. It's called opportunism. Garbage that has been thrown out or discarded becomes valuable if anyone wants it. There are a few boats that sank in the anchorage and are a serious hazard for boating. Nobody wants to remove them because their owners fear that whoever raises them will remove parts and the owner will not get a profit from the salvage, so they just leave them to rot.

The authorities do not enforce the regulations about No Wake Zones inside the marina, and the resulting damage to boats and docks is welcomed as an opportunity to make money with repairs. "Let's do some damage so we can make some money on the repairs" is the idea.

The authorities do enforce the regulations requiring permits, because that is easy money and allows them to exercise their official power and status. Imagine having to pay for a permit to visit some islands without being allowed to set foot on them, or needing a permit to see whales in the ocean.

The people who have these permits think they have the exclusive right to harass the sea life by riding over the animals and causing them injury and death, while at the same time officiously ordering the more responsible boaters who have no permit to go away.

Visitors to Mexico spend a lot of money. If locals want to have an ongoing business with visitors they need to at the very least respect tourists, treat them with courtesy, and protect them from those seeking to take advantage of their ignorance about local conditions and regulations. Otherwise the tourist economy will move on to other places where visitors get better treatment and value for their money.

Chapter 18

RULES

PEOPLE HAVE RULES! I traveled the world, yet somehow this almost escaped my attention. What is really interesting is that the people who insist on rules are the ones that break them. Why is that? Is it to have law and order to make sure all are treated fairly? Is it because they want others to be tied by them while they go about their business? Or is it to have a nice predictable and safe environment to be enjoyed by all?

Don't get me wrong; I'm a staunch non-conformist and delight in breaking rules that make no sense. Why stop for a stop sign when it is absolutely clear to see there is no traffic?

Once I was pulled over by a cop who saw me run a stop sign on my motorcycle in an area as flat as Saskatchewan where one could see on Monday who will visit you on Sunday. He asked me if perhaps I did not see the stop sign? I answered, "I saw that sign but I did not see you. What cow pile did you hide in?"

Two days later I was released from an involuntary visit to the local police station. Just as well, because by then I had finished reading all the philosophical views on the walls left by former visitors and could not contribute with some of my own. That's because among my shoestrings, wallet and other items, the police took my pen, perhaps thinking that I would become suicidal over two days of relaxation in the local zoo and write myself into oblivion.

Early in life it was explained to me that there are rules and they must be followed if we want to have an orderly society. But why does it need to be orderly? Is it to control others, make them predictable, and guide them because otherwise all the idiots will create chaos without end?

If so, we then need "smart" people to become leaders of the poor, wretched masses who can't think for themselves and don't know right from wrong. But people do know these things. So instead of thinking for ourselves we abandon our potential to learn and let the rule makers guide us. "To where?" I ask.

I see no order, peace and fairness in the world as it is today despite all the laws and rules we have. In schools and other institutions we talk to the young people about how rules and laws are to protect us and to guide us in knowing right from wrong and in taking care of each other and our world. But the results we see are not the expected outcome from what has been taught. Could it be that is because of the examples we give with our ways of living? Let's stop treating our children as if they were stupid.

Who and where are these intelligent rulers? I find that any person with some intelligence is able to think for him or herself and does not need to be told what to do.

In looking into rules and laws which try to make all people equal I wonder what would have happened if all those great men and women who contributed so much beauty in art, music and science had conformed to the rules and remained inside the accepted parameters.

Almost the whole world agrees that lawyers, politicians and priests are characters we could do very well without. Why then are we supporting such crap?

I think we surrendered our sense of responsibility and accountability to those people because it is so much easier for us to have someone else responsible and accountable for what's happening. We can then complain about them, point fingers and cry "look what they are doing to us!" Then we go and vote for someone else and guess what, we get the same horse manure with a different face.

I have a theory that goes like this "if someone drives a car safely and knows how to handle it responsibly at any speed in a given circumstance, let him."

How could anyone develop skills in a given field if we stop them before they start? We often talk about prevention and I agree to an extent, but it doesn't mean preventing life so people don't die! Point out the risks and probable cause and effect of an activity, and then give an opportunity to practice it safely until it is mastered, as with learning to drive a car.

We have trainers in all kinds of things so why not train people in life skills in our schools, homes and what have you? Accidents will happen no matter what, but we can reduce them by promoting the development of skills. Such training saved my life when I found myself in a situation where I had to think fast and break the rules to escape a runaway truck with failed brakes.

We need to be accountable if we cause a problem. There are folks who drive according to the rules and have accidents like pearls on a string. Take away their car if they are incapable of managing the vehicle!

Laws and rules only retard the latent skills and potential of people. Common sense is in short supply when we allow others to think for us by regulating our actions. We are the ones who let others run our lives. We do it to ourselves. We hand our power over to them and think we are powerless to make changes.

Of course, now that they have the power to be able to tell us what to do, it is difficult to rise up and resist them. They have the law on their side, or at least try to push their presumed authority in our face. If we resist it, they tell us there are rules. Whoever is in power makes these rules, and when we insist that the rules should apply to them as well, we are seen as unwanted individuals rocking the boat and jeopardizing their position.

Taking back our power will not go smoothly, but fortunately in this chaos of rules and laws we can find some that can be used to neutralize their assumed authority. For instance, just recently I was told that I might not enter the marina with my dinghy because there are people who feel "molested" by the wake my tiny boat creates.

Now it's true that I have complained to no avail about big boats throwing huge wakes as they speed through the marina. I feel that the operators of those boats think it is the way of all seafaring folks to be rocked by waves, and that we would love to feel at home on the rolling sea even in a marina. This isn't the most intelligent conclusion by far, but at least it's logical. So I tried going by the golden rule, "when in Mexico do like the Mexicans". I quickly found out that is a no-no!

It turned out the rules apply only to me when the sign says "maximum 3 knots". This speed limit makes good sense to me, but unfortunately nobody goes 3 knots, more like 8 knots or faster. So when the marina security person approached like a storm trooper, breaking all speed limits on the sidewalk as he pushed through with a belly at least 55 pounds overweight, and leaving a wake of startled tourists scrambling to safety, I braced myself for an impact that was as certain as a donation request in a church.

It arrived with the force of a military tank broadcasting its loud and bullying message in the Spanish language. My limited Spanish vocabulary and comprehension still relies heavily on mimicry, but I quickly deduced that I was being accused of doing something I should not be doing.

It could not be the speed of my dinghy, I reasoned, because almost everyone is in a race around here, so I mistakenly deduced there must be another reason for his attack. With the volume of a bullhorn and a face purple as an eggplant he told me that I molested everybody. I tried to imagine how and what I could possibly have done. I did not see anybody else complaining. So I pointed out to him he was the only one who seems to have been molested because he was by himself.

I suggested that perhaps the problem was because I did not cater to his need to be the authority he would love to be? He then brought up the speed of my dinghy. I countered that everybody speeds in this marina. "Yes" he replied, "but they have a boat in the marina and you don't. This is a private marina, you are not allowed."

"For starters," I responded, "this is a public marina, and many people charter their boats for fishing, whale watching and any kind of tours, so it is more commercial than anything else, but it is run by a Harbor Master who likes to manage it like it was his kingdom and who makes the rules as he sees fit, takes bribes, and if someone questions his authority bullies his way through if he can".

"That is of no interest to me", he fumed. "You can't come here".

"Well, in that case I will have to talk to the Tourist Bureau and tell them about the discrimination that is happening here. I'm still a visitor in this place, like it or not, and if you want to enforce the rules then do it for everybody." He then decided that he had an urgent need to go to the bathroom.

I can't go fast because I don't have a boat in one of their slips? Clearly it's not about the wake, but about the money they get from the slip fees that matters. In truth, I am a believer in a no wake marina and slow down when entering to less than 2 knots, but I wanted to provoke some response because I'm tired of this crap and I can't leave a cup of tea on my table without half of it spilling when they speed by.

They can do what they want, but if you do it to them then you are the bad guy who does not respect the rules. This is how it is in Mexico; if you pay, you can speed, if you don't pay, you have to follow the rules. So for whom are the rules made? Not for the guys with the big bucks because they pay their way out of being accountable, and not for the authorities that use their office to do as they please.

When I told this authority figure that what he is doing is discrimination and he will be reading about it in the local papers, he turned away and looked for something to say, but there was nobody he could ask for help, and I just went about my business and ignored his belligerent attitude.

And this seems to be the prevailing situation all over the world. So here is my question again; who and where are those intelligent and just rulers? The authorities can be clever and even cunning, but intelligent? Intelligent people do not want to be leaders of others, they just want to live their lives as they see fit, and perhaps people follow them, but they will not lead.

Remember that a million blind people may follow a man with only one eye, but the one with only one eye will never follow them. The blind will go where they're told, while the man with one eye can see for himself and choose his own path.

I often feel that we need to take back power from those rulers over people who are being held captive through misinformation, lies, and threats. We chose them to serve the best interests of all the people, but they turned into rulers with their own agenda who think we are here to serve them and their selfish goals. That's not democracy, rather it's self-serving egomania, and we are feeding it by electing them, even though we hate doing it.

We bitch and talk about it all the time, wasting energy and feeding the thing we don't want, instead of focusing the same energy on what we do want. And like Henry Ford said, "if you think you can or you can't, you're right." So it's better to think positively about what we want. We all have the power to change things for the better if we change our focus from what we don't want to what we do want.

Situations will always come up to challenge our wits. When we take the circumstances as they are without losing sight of what we want, the situation will dissolve and reshape itself to offer an opportunity that was hidden until our positive attitude caused further development.

Some co-workers and I had just finished a painting job in a new building, and as we packed up our tools one of the guys punched a hole in the drywall with a ladder in a location that we would have to totally redo to make the repair invisible. The spot was narrow and hard to get at, with light coming in from a ceiling window, so any unevenness would be obvious. I decided to cut a hole bigger than the accidental one, make a frame fitting into the cutout, install some glass shelves, and stain and varnish the whole thing. It looked fantastic! Sometimes we are so fixed on an idea, we cannot see how much better things can be done until we let go of the old idea and allow ourselves to see things differently.

I saw somewhere a play with words that pointed out where you place the "C" makes the difference between REACTING and CREATING. Often we use words like "should" and "have to", and neither one leaves much room for creativity. Life is not a "should be" affair and "have to" is not our choice, it's a situation forced upon us.

Imagine hearing a person saying, "I have to see my wife". I would not want to be in his wife's place if he does not want to see her but has to. Not much love there. It would be far more pleasant to make our choices because we want to, and not because we have to do things.

And that is the trouble with laws. They are things that are forced upon us, things that we really do not choose but are chosen for us by others according to their points of view, in an attempt to make all of us equal. But people are not equal. Every person has a different point of view, taste, level of intelligence and preference. How can we expect everyone to follow one idea?

Allow others to live their lives as they want, and as long as it does not physically interfere with or limit your life it's okay. That's the only rule we need to live by, unless we want to be rulers over others.

Chapter 19

POVERTY

poverty (noun)

1. the state of not having enough money to take care of basic needs such as food, clothing, and housing

2. a deficiency or lack of something

3. lack of soil fertility or nutrients

NOT BEING ABLE to meet basic needs is bad enough, but it's even worse if you have a big appetite. And it seems the majority of humans have an insatiable appetite for things.

First I became aware of this when we arrived in West Germany in 1957 after our escape from Hungary. I could not speak the German language, but I made some friends, and we either played soccer or played cowboys and Indians after school. I mostly played the role of a redskin.

I had often dreamed about living with horses, free like the wind, and roaming the Puszta (Hungarian for Prairie) where the expanse was so vast that on Wednesday you could see from the Sunday behind you to the Sunday ahead, and didn't have to go to church.

The cowboys had guns strapped around their waists, hats on their heads, and a star on their vests. I had a naked upper body, coal paint on my face, and a loincloth over my underwear. I had a stick that was either a rifle or spear depending on need. My mind was also a weapon, one that enabled me to dig traps, lay trip wires and hide in plain sight. I learned to be a savage at an early age, and enjoyed it.

My cowboy friends thought I was an Indian because I was poor and could not afford a cowboy outfit. They also got colds at least twice a year and did what the white man had done to the red man, gave the flu in exchange for his land.

After killing, mutilating and massacring me, my friends thanked God for his help in getting rid of the heathen wild savages and invited me to watch TV with them, because that was the right thing to do after you have killed your enemy. No one should have to die without the chance to watch TV after death (today's programs will finish you off for good!)

I really enjoyed watching a show where a little guy armed only with an umbrella and his wits fought guys with guns and muscles, and won. I was fascinated to see pictures like the movies in a small box.

Then my friend asked me why we didn't have a TV. I didn't know why we should have one, after all they had one, and many of us were able to watch it. But he said it belonged to them, and if we had one too then we didn't have to watch theirs. What was his point? We were together and had a good time and did not harm the TV by looking at it. Then he said the word "youarepoorandcannotaffordatv".

Until then I had never felt poor, not even in Hungary when we had nothing to eat for two weeks. We felt hungry, but not poor. So I told my father that we were poor because we did not have a TV. He bought one. We were rich. A few years later we were poor again because we did not have a color TV. And so we were poor in a country that had everything and we didn't. It seemed like we would never ever have enough, because there was always more to be had.

We were poor for many years, but still today I don't know what it feels like to be poor. I felt hungry, thirsty, angry, cheated, betrayed, deserted, to name some of the things that I consider bad feelings, but how does it feel to be poor?

I own a sailing yacht that many rich people envy me for. It is not big, though a boat 11.65m in length is plenty enough space for a couple. These rich people tell me how they wish for a lifestyle like I have, but say they could never afford it. They have millions, so why not? I'm broke most of the time to the point where I cannot even pay attention, so why would they, with all the money they have, feel that they would not be able to afford it? Do they feel poor?

How must it feel like to have all that money and not be able to afford a lifestyle like mine? Somehow that money or the way they manage it must make them feel poor. Maybe it is greed that causes them to think and feel there will never be enough to afford a lifestyle that is free from the feeling of poverty. Poor rich man. The Buddhists say, "True happiness is wanting what you have, not having what you want."

Could it be that this sense of poverty experienced by the wealthy has its roots in the need to prove to others that they are worthy of respect and love? What and to whom do they have to prove anything? Are they slaves to their possessions? I found out long ago; I don't own things. They own me. It seems the key to wealth is the ability to let go of attachments. We may use things, and with the purchase of them we earn the right to do so, but that should not put us in bondage to them.

In my life I have moved from one house to another, and for a while each was my place it seemed, but when I moved out it became someone else's. I used it for a time, but it was not mine.

All things I touch can be taken from me in the snap of a finger, but the things that really matter nobody can take. Love, wisdom, knowledge and experience are what we acquire things with. But we are so attached to things that we even call children, husbands, wives and friends "ours", overlooking the fact that they are with us, not for us. What makes us rich is the ability to experience all that life offers, the love we have for such experience, the wisdom to accept it, and the knowledge of how to use it.

My childhood in Hungary and Germany was a great preparation for my future outlook on life, and how I look at fairness and justice. I understood that it was not important to own things, but rather to share them with others. That way we all took responsibility for something's maintenance, and enjoyed an afternoon together after the war game was over. Us redskins were treated to TV and snacks after our torments, the cowboys had their share of bruises, and justice was handed out when they had to accompany their parents to church while we Indians hid in the woods. Who says there is no god?

I felt no poverty then, and now in Mexico I see people who claim to be poor by North American standards but who laugh a lot. Their children seem to be happy with the things they get, but when they grow up the same poverty-stricken expression sets in on their faces that I see on rich people who have everything. I think that wanting more is the problem, and it creates a feeling of being poor. To me, the distance between what we have and what we wish for determines the degree of our unhappiness and poverty.

I remember learning this lesson well when I first encountered my feelings for the opposite sex. In my youth there was a goddess in her glory, who played a murderous flirting game with all my friends. There was nobody who did not want to suffer and die for her. Our fantasies had no limits. In less than two minutes we went through all possible scenarios from courtship to divorce by beheading.

You probably know the game "spin the bottle". We played that game on days when the goddess was around, and it became an obsession with me. My friends knew of my affection and teased me by calling her to play. Due to my newly discovered "poverty" I did not have the courage to ask her out, and I didn't even consider myself worthy to participate in the game.

I had nothing of value to offer and so remained in the background, while all the guys had a good time and enjoyed kissing the girl who was in my fantasies 26 hours a day. (I borrowed the two extra hours from the end of my life!) Then the incredible happened; the bottle pointed to me through a gap that opened temporarily when one of the boys shifted his position.

I nearly fainted from the joy and the fear that sprang up like a grasshopper. My heart stuck in my throat. All eyes were on me, but hers were the only ones that I noticed. I read a mixture of panic and fear and what I thought to be repulsion. I could not move, and someone shoved me toward her with the words "We're waiting. Hurry up!" What they were waiting for I'll never know, but when she just kissed me on the forehead, I felt the whole world collapsing and the entire weight of it crushing me.

How I made it home remains an unknown accomplishment. My face was still there, but something was wrong with the mirror, because it looked distorted and my eyes were swimming in a lake. The humiliation of rejection paralyzed me, and I thought it must have something to do with the situation of being poor.

Shortly after we moved to another town and I was spared the agony of seeing her go out with one of my friends, who became the god we all wanted to be. Years later I met her again and she looked incredible, still single and working as a photo model for a clothing company. I was not as shy as when I was younger. I asked her out for a movie and she agreed. We met two hours before the show, and while having a bite to eat our conversation came to that game with the bottle.

To my question as to why she had only kissed me on the forehead, she replied: "You were always different from the other guys, and not very popular because of the way you talk and act. I knew you liked me, and I liked you too, but I enjoyed the attention of all the guys and did not want to be seen hanging out with you and thought to be as weird as you."

This didn't make me feel all that much better, but at least it was a relief to know that it had nothing to do with me not having money or things. I relaxed, and from then on we were friends, and if it wasn't for the fact I had a girlfriend at the time, who knows what would have happened.

So it seems to me that the image of poverty is only in our mind, where it affects our behavior by stifling our creativity and drive for adventure. We like to believe that other countries that have less than us are poor and need our help. This makes us feel good, rather than the people we degrade with our gifts.

It's been said, "the easiest way to keep a beggar a beggar is to give to him". Giving allows us to feel superior by demonstrating our "goodness". It is the ultimate humiliation of others. It is not poverty that people fear (if they still have some dignity left) so much as the condescending attitude of "the good Samaritan". And giving is condescending, most ways you look at it.

You may recall the proverb "if I give you fish today, you have something to eat for today. If I teach you how to fish, you have fish every day." Old sayings are old because they have enduring truth in them.

Poverty exists only in rich people's minds and in the minds of those who want more, other people just work to live, and don't think much about it. There is no shame in not having more than what is needed to live, but we are not satisfied with that. So we hoard large quantities of money, food or things for future use, and then we die howling that we have not used these things while living.

While there are no limits to greed, there is a limit for moderation. The art of living is about how little you can make do with, not about how much. Any idiot can live with a lot, but only the wise know how little is needed. I have a sailboat, and some people look at it and think I must be stinking rich. They have a house, a car, TV, video and stereo equipment that would blast holes in the fabric of the universe, yet they envy me for my boat and think I'm rich?

The boat is all I have as far as things go. I don't have a car, nor a house with three bedrooms, kitchen, bathrooms, storage, garage, patio and backyard. But I live free, and go when and where I want, for as long as I like. I work where I am, and when I need money. When I want a change of scenery, I cast off the lines or weigh anchor and move. No packing things and discovering all that junk that I once thought I would use one day, and no real estate problems.

When you own a house that house is yours. When you own a boat the whole world is yours. You don't have to own a lot of things to enjoy them, and you may remain poor and yet be rich.

I took a lot of people sailing without getting paid for it, and made friends. When I needed assistance they came to my aid, even with money. Some took off time from their busy schedule to transport an engine to the repair shop, others lent me money to get repairs done, and some carried parts through customs at the risk of being accused of smuggling.

Money is not as important as we like to think. You are rich when you have friends. So learn how to make friends and how to be a friend. You will be surprised how much people value real friendship, because there is not much of it around anymore. We often buy "friendship" because it's easier than to earn friendship, but how enduring is that? We all know the answer.

Cultivating friendships is where wealth is found in mutual support and in assistance to get out of a difficult situation. When help is necessary, it should only be used when there are no other options to assist. The word help implies that the other cannot get out of the situation on his or her accord, and in helping we must take care not to come across as acting superior.

A good way is to ask for something in return that the other can do. That would allow them to retain their dignity, and after they recovered we may ask for the balance owing, if there is any. Otherwise we are maintaining the thought and condition of poverty out of a need to feel good about ourselves when we give. It releases us from feeling guilty about having what they do not, since by giving we can say that we are doing our best to eliminate poverty without realizing that we are in fact perpetuating it.

Why in the world would anyone want to work when you get it for free? All one needs to do is look poor and hold up a can and someone comes along and drops in money to release some of their guilt. I have heard people say that they would be stupid to work for minimum wages when they get more from welfare for doing nothing.

One day I wanted to find out how it feels to be begging for food or money, and stopped shaving for a few days and avoided washing, much to my discomfort. Within three days I smelled like a bear. Then I sat momentarily on the curb of a busy thoroughfare, before I was chased away by another scruffy looking individual who owned that section of the street. After a while one of the street people took pity on me and told me to go home and clean up. He did not buy my act.

I explained to him what I wanted to do. He then offered the information I sought, for a price. That would not do, so I insisted that he let me do my own begging. Finally he agreed to rent me a section of his street. For a week I begged for money and food, and for advice from my rental agent on how to make money. He never told me, but volunteered to give me some insight into his own income per week. It turned out to be more than I made when I was working as a painter for an outfit in Vancouver!

When I expressed doubt, he gave me a demonstration. He approached a car with a woman sitting inside getting ready to go shopping. He changed his behavior to that of a subservient person, and became a helpless "invalid" in an instant. I would not have recognized him if I had not known him for a week.

I could not hear what he was saying, but after three minutes or less he came back and tossed me a twenty-dollar bill. "Keep it" he said. "I'll get some more. Wait here." With that he left and I decided to get a coffee. When I returned to my section, he was there, took my coffee and showed me another ten-dollar bill.

Looking at the money I wondered how in the world he did that. "You got to act, man!" His acting was good enough to go to Hollywood. "I could stroke easy $500 a day without sweat, but I don't do coke and I work only four hours. Tops" he said.

By comparison I earned $120 for eight hours work as a painter. He may have been an exception, but he charged me $100 a day for sitting on my butt and collecting hemorrhoids and change. That is an untapped income tax source bureaucrats would love to know about!

Poverty is a perception from the outside. It is a slogan that can be exploited, like anything else. It is all business. Poverty is not humanitarian, but it says a lot about humanity.

Chapter 20

TERRORISM

I'M NOT SURE if my cat has any political connections or affiliations to the local Taliban, IRA or Al Fattah but there is a possibility she has connections with local bombers and assassins. If she is politically motivated it hasn't surfaced yet, but it is evident that she has an agenda.

I acquired her as a playmate for my male cat-friend, who, I thought in my deluded mind, needed one. I went to the local adopt-a-pet (it would be more appropriate to call it the "adopt-a-terrorist" shop) and there was this innocent looking, big-eyed, purring and face-licking hairball, which apparently could not make up its mind if it was going to be white, red, grey or tabby and instead became all.

I got suckered in by her charms and in my trusting way paid the adoption fee and proceeded to take her to her new home and introduce her to my cat-friend Csiko, who I hoped would not be too harsh with her. He wasn't. She was!

I should have smelled a rat when I put the fuzzy thing on my shoulder and rode the bicycle toward the marina, and she put daggers concealed in satin paws into my back when a cab roared past us. The friendly doctor who surgically removed the kitten from me wondered if anyone had ever given birth to a kitten through the ribs before. He had heard a story about a woman fashioned from the ribs of a guy named Adam, but a cat had never been mentioned. This was a first for both of us.

On the boat things soon became clear. Csiko was no longer allowed to reside on the boat. There was a hissing and growling going on that would scare the wits out of a tiger, and Csiko reluctantly ceded ground to the fury of teeth and claws and the sound wave that followed.

It didn't matter much that Csiko was first on the boat and had all the privileges that one earned over time. This assault was not anything he had anticipated, so he did not return to the boat, and demonstrated his disapproval in a way only cats know how to do.

Whenever I called him before the arrival of Miss Kitty, he used to answer me. When he returned from a night on the town, he announced his return with a meow loud enough to wake me from deep slumber, and snuggled into my arm and pawed my face with soft caress.

Now he did not even come home. When I saw him ashore, he just looked and then turned away like a scorned woman. Then with a twitch of his tail he would saunter off into the thicket, without another glance in my direction.

Guilt flooded my heart, and I contemplated returning the kitten to the shop and making up with Csiko by buying the juiciest fish I could find, and letting him gorge himself. But then I thought that if I just gave them more time, they would get over their mutual dislike and all would be well.

Oh, how female felines so easily foil the hopes of man. Csiko knew that this kitten was set in her ways. She was born to be a single-minded terrorist, and living proof that you can't always negotiate with them.

With this kitten no gentle handling was possible. She was always in attack mode, and when I broke away from her claws and teeth by brute force, her hissing and growling was such that I was afraid to let her out of my grasp lest she ripped me to shreds.

Csiko the wise showed better sense by staying away and letting me take the brunt of her attacks. On the rare occasions when he showed up near the boat to check on the situation and see if I was still alive, he would look from the cover of the bushes toward the boat, then like a ninja vanish into thin air.

How wrong I was in thinking that in a few days the situation would resolve into a happy ever after! A month later, Csiko finally condescended to visit at a time when he figured the snarling, hissing ball of fur was sleeping. As soon as he jumped onto the boat, I eased the lines and moved a bit forward to get away from the wall where he could retreat.

As long as I was around to take the first line of defense against the kitten, he was able to have a few bites of the food that was there before taking off again. But with the boat now further from the wall, that escape route was gone and he had to find sanctuary somewhere else. Alas, on a boat you can run but you cannot hide, and Csiko found out very fast how true that is.

The gel paint coating on my deck was wearing thin from their chasing around. When I got off the boat to have some peace on-shore, Csiko jumped into the water and swam to the dock to escape. If you know cats and their phobia for getting wet, you will understand how desperate he must have felt.

One day a heard a splash near the boat, and thinking it could have been a large fish jumping, ignored it. Then I heard a wailing that was like something in a horror movie. I try to write the sound but it will not do justice. yoauuu! I jumped up from the table and raced into the cockpit to see a wet pussy, with eyes as big as dishes, floating near the transom of the boat and frantically trying to get back onboard.

For a moment I thought, (shame on me) this is the answer to my prayers and the solution to all of our problems, but my humanitarian side broke surface and I put my arm into the water. The kitten clawed on in an instant and scaled my arm like a monkey up onto my head, then jumped off onto the deck.

Cussing and yowling like the kitten as I spurted blood like a fountain, I grabbed a towel hanging on the lifelines as if placed there for just this purpose. Wrapping the towel around my arm and neck in an attempt to staunch the bleeding before I died without first having a chance to kill the cat I chased after her.

Miss Kitty, sensing her imminent doom, elected the only strategy that could save her. She looked at me, her eyes still big and round like saucer cups, and let out a mournful wailing sound that made me forget all thought of murder.

Disregarding the fact I was bleeding to death, I picked up the soaking fur ball that was Miss Kitty, and wrapped her in the towel to dry her off. I'm not sure if it was fear or being wet that made her shiver, but she was vibrating all over. As I dried her she pushed her head into my armpit as if she wanted to take cover from a mad bulldog. My heart melted and compassion overpowered my excellent reasons for killing this mortal enemy.

"Oh, what a sweet kitten this is," was all I could think. "Poor thing, so scared and cold and salty. Ah! Salty! She needs a warm rinse to get her to warm up and get rid of the salt. Into the head with her". But oh, what a mistake that was. Never in my life did I see anything so fast, accurate and powerful escaping the head compartment through a porthole. She must have had the best Ninja warrior training that has been developed since the Shogun in Japan.

Miss Kitty has never forgiven me that treacherous attempt to alleviate her salty cat status. Whenever I have a shower and enter the salon to sit down, she attacks and bites whatever body parts she can reach. The bites are no longer as vicious as they were in the first few weeks because I had to restrain her a few times with considerable force, but she still gets me when I'm lowering my guard.

She also has developed a technique to get me when I'm sleeping and bites my arm, chest or any other part of my body that she can get at, even if she has to pull the blanket off me to do so.

We recently made a truce that seems to be holding. When I encounter her on my pillow I pet her and after the initial customary biting and clawing she settles down and even snuggles up to me for a few minutes. The truce hinges on a little hard rubber ball that she is very fond of. It bounces and she chases it all over the boat, hides it in my berth and has a blast when I toss it for her to chase. When she has had her way with it, she brings it to me so I can show her what else to do with it.

I can't get rid of the suspicion that she just wants to put me at ease before striking me down. So far so good though. Often when I return to the boat she greets me on deck and rubs herself on me as if I was her favorite toy, which may very well be the case.

I wonder when she will try to recruit me for her hidden agenda. So far she has not demanded anything worse than to catch a fish, kill it and let her eat it. But I fear in the near future she will tell me to take the fish hostage and exchange them for imprisoned cats around the world that have been impounded for obscure reasons. I believe I could be talked into that, and hope it will not escalate into an all-out war with slogans like "death to all humans". My hope is that she is more humane than humans. And what does a little suffering matter among friends? Now as time has gone by, this kitten has grown into an almost adult cat and there is a reconciliation process happening between Csiko and her that include my First Mate and me. Miss Kitty visits us in bed, where she is plotting her sinister plan to overthrow the human race.

Irma has a fondness for her; it must be a female thing. They spend hours together that I could consider eerie, were it not for the genuine affection and authentic being of my mate. I assume that it is my getting close to agreeing with the ideologies these two females represent that allows me to live in relative peace.

We four are sharing a harmonious and symbiotic space by having learned to live with each other. If we can do that there is hope that others in the world can learn from our animal nature and create a better world. In such a world all can live in peace and love without the need to convert or force our views on others.

If we all can learn to respect our differences and see them as flowers of all kinds and not want to create a "Read my Lips" only world, we could at least have a better understanding of others, even if we do not agree with their ways. We can rest in peace knowing that they will not agree with our ways either, if they don't want to.

By allowing ourselves to observe and to be observed, we may discover that others have ways to see the world that we do not, and these ways may be better than our thoughts. We call this attitude open-ness to change. It is amazing how the statement "I know" has closed our minds and created rigidity in our being that is foul and stagnant.

It is time to re-think our ways of thinking and acting because they have brought us to the brink of destruction. If we want to survive as a species, we must re-create our ways. Thinking for us would be a step in the right direction. Sharing the world with another and respecting our differences is a good second step, and to add some spice let's work on our sense of humor about ourselves.

Taking our achievements and us too seriously creates a sense of self-importance that has made life all over this planet a zest pool of greed, disrespect and a struggle for supremacy over others. Focusing instead on things that makes us and everybody around us feel good can change the world for the better.

Chapter 21

SAILOR'S BLUES

SOME FEEL A deep reverence for love. Others may think of it as a four-letter word. Many exploit it. Some run from it. Others run toward and fall for it. Running too fast into love is like colliding with a train. It hurts, although for a masochist such pain may be enjoyable. Others just pussy-foot around and play with love. There is something about it that attracts humans (or those who think they are) like flies to the sweet smell of rotting fruit. I am not talking about the love that is heavenly or talked about in some sacred books and scriptures.

I am talking about down to earth every day just-for-the-fun-because-there-is-nothing-else-to-do rutting. We sailors are not exempt from this love effect, in fact we are suckers for it. Could this be because we spend a lot of time tinkering with the boat that is the object of our devotion, and when we take a break we realize that we've been missing being loved in return?

So what are we going to do? We go to a restaurant, or the local watering hole, whether a bar, or a coffee shop and begin, timidly or boldly, looking around for a sympathetic smile, someone who may also be looking for some diversion. Looks are important, but willingness is a must. Forget intelligence, because an intelligent person won't get involved without thoroughly getting to know you first.

On my part conversation is always about the boat; the work of a sailor, the pleasures of sailing, how much fun a boat can be, and how much aggravation it can cause. The chosen subject may not grasp half the meaning so listens with just half an ear, but is mesmerized by the torrent of words spilling from a sailor's mouth.

Once we have the subject's attention, we give an account of our adventures that makes us look like heroes. Now we are getting somewhere. Here is a chance to shine and show our romantic and adventurous side as we relate how the waves were sky high and we stood watch over the vessel and our crew, climbed the mast in a wild, raging storm, and bested the elements to emerge in one piece, and just a bit exhausted. There's not much to brag about in calm seas, or during sunset or sunrise, or while spending day-in and day-out sitting at the helm with nothing else to do except watch the swells slowly lifting and lowering the vessel in a never-ending rhythm.

It is astonishing how our sailing stories affect others. They invite us for lunch or pay for our coffee or beer. When we have managed to impress them sufficiently we may even get a chance to spend a night with them, but mostly only with one at a time.

And here comes the part that creates the problems. In our deluded way of thinking we believe that the other loves us. On occasion they may even think they are in love, but in reality they are far from it. They have been just as lonely for company as us. We entertain them sufficiently and create a romantic illusion for them, but when we run out of stories and want to create some more, they will not want to be a subject in those stories.

When the real adventure begins they prefer to hear about it, but not to be part of it. It is much safer to watch the movie "Perfect Storm" with real surround sound, from an armchair, while munching a snack from the fixed solid fridge, and while sipping on a beverage without the heaving deck causing the drinker to wear it. What is really funny this people sitting in their armchair, one hand white-knuckled clinging to the armrest while chewing on the fingernails on the other hand and getting scared in front of the TV. The chance to drown while drinking on solid ground is minimal, and walking to the fridge for another one is not the dangerous trip it is in a gale at sea.

In addition, the daily chores on boats are overwhelming. In order to fill on-board tanks with water or fuel I must either use the dinghy, fill up the containers, return to the vessel, heave the load aboard and fill up the tanks, or else go to the fuel dock, pay an arm and a leg for the stuff, and then pay the docking fee.

I take the cheaper alternative. What the hell, its good exercise walking two miles in scorching heat three times with two jerry cans holding 5 gallons each. Afterwards my arms are so stretched I can touch my toes without bending, and dragging my knuckles on the ground also explains the dirty fingernails. People with weight problems would benefit from this. Now imagine doing laundry. Asking your mate to assist you with chores is like inviting a mutiny, so it is up to the captain to do all the heavy work. Throwing yourself overboard is not an option, as the captain can't abandon ship.

Telling a story is great because of the effect it has on an audience. With oral embellishment we can be five star hotel gourmet cooks concocting a wonderful dining experience from the contents of our boat's larder. This makes for a cheap night for us and costly for the others, but people should expect to pay for being entertained.

Then there is the ongoing f.o.r.d. work (fix or repair daily). Hanging upside-down in a near inaccessible cramped, hot, and dirty engine room, or in a cabin that is so small you have to step outside if you want to change your mind, is a breeding ground for combinations of four letter words that are limited only by one's imagination.

Other factors contributing to our blues are necessary repairs and the associated down time. We all have plenty of our own versions of that chapter. If we happen to have lured someone onto our boat during repair times they need to be very much in love with us to stay. A lot of extracurricular romantic activity is advisable, and even that is no guarantee of a happy outcome.

It is amazing how boats can accelerate the natural process of relationship difficulties at least a hundred fold. Something that may not have surfaced for fifty years can pop up in just a few months, even with the benefit of having shore leave more frequently than on the high seas. Who would want to live a lifestyle like that?

Our honeys are soon getting cabin fever syndrome, and coming up with stories of their own to escape the nautical environment. Perhaps they need to take care of family members who are in need of a third eye transplant, a second liver, or a new growth of hair on their chest. Others find it necessary to find a job in a kingdom far, far away to earn money, and make promises to return when things are better. They want to remain friends, because one never knows.

Well, here we are, the poor dregs of a barrel of wine turned vinegar, with a long face that could be mistaken for a cowboy's old horse, wondering what happened to the "love forever" and "soul-mates since time immemorial". Sailors are suckers for romantic movies, stories and songs because they recognize their own life in them. It's a blues that most of us could sing but I would be hard pressed to find any other species than sailors susceptible to so much disillusion.

In all harbors I have met sailors, males and females who had stories that would make a stone cry, yet it did not make them calloused for romance, and their eyes still had a sparkle that made them attractive and alive looking. There must be something in this sailing lifestyle that is keeping them young, curious and interesting. That may be the reason some want it for a while, until the hardships of this kind of life gets to be too much for the average person, and they look for an easier life that is less demanding on them.

When they move on, they leave behind a confused sailor who would like to understand what the hell people do not like about a life on the sea that gives them skills, knowledge, self-confidence, freedom, a deeper understanding of all that is and a sense of awe about human potential.

We want to share such opportunity with those less fortunate land-dwellers. They have gotten used to living on the land for such a long time that they forgot we all came from the sea in our genetic beginnings, and feel dismayed when they do not want to go or are afraid to go on the oceans as many others do. It is only a matter of getting used to life on a boat, and it is not a disability to do so.

Maybe there is a silver lining in the clouds once we reach the horizon, but for me the end of the water is always just out of reach.

To be continued.